BEHOLD HIS GLORY

Behold
His
GLORY

Encountering God
Through the
Meaning of His Names

ALETHA HINTHORN

Beacon Hill Press of Kansas City
Kansas City, Missouri

Copyright 2001
by Aletha Hinthorn

ISBN 083-411-8793

Printed in the
United States of America

Cover Design: Ted Ferguson

10   9   8   7   6   5   4   3   2   1

CONTENTS

PREFACE

"I AM here for you." These words came to me early one Saturday morning. Two days earlier I had finished a first draft of this book, and although I had written each chapter hoping to express some aspect of God's goodness, I had not thought of one phrase that perfectly captured what I wanted to say in these pages.

Then came these words: "I am here for you," and I recalled their significance. God appeared to Moses in the burning bush and commissioned him to lead the people of Israel out of Egypt. Moses protested, "If I go to the people of Israel and tell them, 'The God of your ancestors has sent me to you,' they won't believe me. They will ask, 'Which god are you talking about? What is his name?' Then what should I tell them?" (Exod. 3:13, NLT).

God replied, "I AM WHO I AM" (v. 14).

What kind of an answer was God giving Moses? According to William Dyrness in *Themes in Old Testament Theology,* the best translation would be: "I will be there, as I am here" or "I am here for you."[1] God was assuring His people of His presence. No other god did that!

What difference does it make when we live aware of His continual attentive presence? A lady in her 80s told me, "I just love growing old because I become more and more aware of this wonderful presence with me." The more aware we are of His presence, the more we realize that He is continually within us to do us good. His love and attentiveness exceed that of every human relationship, even that of a mother with her small baby.

Throughout that Saturday, I continued to hear these words, "I am here for you." As the impact of what it means to have the Almighty God say that not only is He within me but He is here to meet my every need, I realized there could be only one appropriate response. Again and again my heart responded, "I am here for You! I have no desire in life except to give You glory."

This awesome presence is not a reality to be taken for granted. It is one to pursue relentlessly, and when we do, we discover as David did that there is only one thing in life worthy of our passion. "One thing I ask of the LORD, this is what I seek . . . to gaze upon the beauty of the LORD" (Ps. 27:4).

With all our hearts, Lord, we seek to behold Your glory.

INTRODUCTION

A SPEAKER lecturing on creativity at a Kansas City editors' meeting asked the audience, "How many of you get messages from the universe besides me? The other day I saw a little lid on the ground that said, 'Shake well.' I picked it up and carried it around with me for a few days and realized it was telling me to be a creative maverick."

Her words reveal the universal heart longing for a word from the Eternal One. Yet if we are to know anything about God it will be because He reveals himself to us. "Canst thou by searching find out God?" (Job 11:7, KJV). The *New Living Translation* states this verse, "Can you discover everything there is to know about the Almighty?" Such knowledge is higher than the heavens." If communion with God is to be possible, then He must reveal to us what He is like. Amazingly, He longs to reveal himself to us.

His Glory Is His Goodness

"I want to see God," cried five-year-old Hannah. Her mother could have responded by saying, "Hannah, there are two different ways to see others. We can see their physical bodies and notice if they are tall, short, handsome, or blond. Or we can see them by observing their spirits. Are they kind, loving, and gentle, or are they harsh and unkind? Seeing someone's spirit is the most important way to see someone. This is the way God allows us to see Him. He wants us to know what His Spirit is like."

At the close of His natural life, Jesus spoke about both ways of seeing Him. "Before long, the world will not see me anymore, but you will see me" (John 14:19). His physical body would not be visible much longer, but those who learn to behold His Spirit with their spirits would continue to see Him.

When Moses longed to see God, he prayed, "Now show me your glory" (Exod. 33:18). He wanted to know God in His essence. This nuance is captured in the Septuagint, which says, "Show me thyself." He wanted to know God's nature.

God can never resist such a longing, but how would He respond to Moses' plea? Would He show him a physical form? Would He break a cedar and show him His power? Would He display His wisdom to show He is omniscient?

No, Moses had a revelation of God's good Spirit: "I will cause all my goodness to pass in front of you" (v. 19). When we see God's glory, we see His goodness. God's greatest glory is that He is good. Dyrness insists that when God promises to show His glory in Exod. 16:7, "the meaning is that Moses and the people will see his care."[1]

Michael Horton states in his book *In the Face of God* that God's glory is not communicated through a flash of experience that cannot be explained in words: "Quite the contrary, God insists that his glory could only be seen through words."[2] If we want to experience God's glory, it is "a glorious revelation of God himself as good and gracious."[3]

Using This Book

At the beginning of each chapter that considers some aspect of God's goodness (chapters 2 through 9), we will briefly consider one of the names of God. It is of great significance that God disclosed His name to us, because to know someone's name is to have a relationship with that person. God wants us to have an intimate relationship with Him, so He revealed himself through many names. A new crisis among His people often caused God to describe himself with a new name. It was as if He said, "Now you can call Me by this name," and the new name always spoke to their new situation.

The second small section in each of these eight chapters focuses on Jesus. When Christ said that He had come in His Father's name, He meant He was to be heard as the Father (John 5:43). "The Son is the radiance of God's glory and the exact representation of his being" (Heb. 1:3). Jesus shares God's glory, not merely as a reflector, but as the radiance or manifestation. "The Word became flesh and made his dwelling among us. We have seen his glory, the glory of the One and Only, who came from the Father, full of grace and truth" (John 1:14).

The remainder of these chapters will focus on some aspect of God's glory. I pray that through these pages, God will once again cause His goodness to pass in front of us.

As we continue looking at Christ, His image will be reproduced in us.

*Glory is the weight of
God's worthiness.*

1

ʃHOW Uʃ YOUR GLORY!

AN EDITOR of a secular women's magazine surveyed the top 10 women's magazines and reported that the two top topics in them are how to stay thin and how to stay young. She titled her talk "Let Them Read Fluff." Fluff is all that is left when we remove Truth. When nothing about God is revealed, all, as Solomon came to realize, is meaningless.

Glory comes from a root whose meaning is "heavy." If you have ever been where God's presence is revealed, you understand this definition. I recall a church service in which a couple sang "Worthy Is the Lamb," and a holy hush descended. God's presence seemed so real that for moments after the singing, no one, including the singers, moved. We all sat lost in the glory of His presence.

The glory of God is an expression of His stunning importance and reality. It is a quality of God's character that emphasizes His greatness and authority. Most of all, His glory is His awesome love expressing itself.

Let's consider what God's glory looked like to those in the Old Testament and how we behold His glory now. Then we will look at some who received special revelations of God, and finally consider what is necessary for us to behold His glory.

What Is His Glory?

1. When God appeared to Old Testament observers, it was His glory, His overwhelmingly majestic reality, that impressed them. Read the following occurrences and record phrases that describe His glory.

Exod. 24:17

Deut. 5:24

1 Kings 8:11

Ezek. 1:28

Imagine being an ancient Israelite, stepping out of your tent, looking over toward the Tabernacle, and viewing a fiery, cloudy pillar—God's Shechinah glory. You could turn to your child and say, "See that fiery pillar? God is still with us!" God's glory was a visible reality to the Israelites.

Although the term *Shechinah* is not in the Bible, the rabbis used the term frequently in their literature to describe the visible presence of God. This luminous cloud of transcendent brightness appeared as the pillar of cloud and fire that hovered above the Tabernacle and led the children of Israel in their journeys. It rested on the most holy place.[1]

2. The following verses describe the cloud by day and the pillar of fire by night. Consider what this symbol of God's presence showed the Israelites about God's care and concern.

Exod. 13:21-22

Exod. 14:19-25

Exod. 33:7-11

Num. 9:15-23

Neh. 9:12, 19-21

Ps. 78:14

Ps. 99:7

Ps. 105:39

Shechinah is from a root meaning "dwelling." The rabbis taught that the divine presence, the Shechinah glory, brings God to dwell with us so closely He even shares our sorrows.

They said, "During the time that [God's people are] in trouble, what language does the Shechinah employ? 'I have a heaviness in My head; I have a heaviness in My arms.'"[2] They viewed the Shechinah as a compassionate presence.

We now understand the Shechinah glory in the Hebrew Bible to metaphorically speak of the second person of the Trinity. The reality symbolized by the fiery pillar is the indwelling presence of Jesus Christ. "Christ in you, the hope of glory," exclaimed Paul in Col. 1:27. All that God's presence was to the Israelites, Christ longs to be to each of us. Jesus came to make God's glory visible to us.

Rabbinical literature often depicted the Shechinah as light. For instance, the phrase, "The earth did shine with His glory" received the comment, "This is the face of the Shechinah."[3]

3. How did Jesus identify himself in John 8:12?

4. Notice the description of Jesus Christ in Heb. 1:3.

5. Heb. 1:3 in the *Amplified Bible* provides a picture of Jesus as the Shechinah glory: "He is the sole expression of the glory of God [the Light-being, the out-raying or radiance of the divine], and He is the perfect imprint and very image of [God's] nature."

Because Jesus could always say, "I seek not to please myself but him who sent me" (John 5:30), the writer to the Hebrews could say, "The Son is the radiance of God's glory" (1:3).

If John had not written that Isaiah "saw Jesus' glory" (John 12:41), we might not recognize that many of Isaiah's references to future glory refer to Jesus. One example is in 49:3: "You are My servant . . . in Whom I will show My glory" (NASB). Also see Isa. 60:1.

6. Let's consider a few of the verses that associate God's glory with Jesus.
Luke 9:28-32
John 2:11
1 Cor. 2:8
2 Cor. 4:4, 6

7. What was the Old Testament promise regarding this glory as given in Isa. 40:5?

8. Has this promise been fulfilled? See John 1:14.

9. Jesus came to reveal God's glory to us. Compare Isa. 49:6 with Luke 2:32. About who were Simeon and Isaiah speaking?

10. God's glory includes all His attributes—all His goodness! Let's consider the ways in which Jesus, the second person of the Trinity, is "the exact representation of his being" (Heb. 1:3) and so to look at Him is to see God's glory. God is
    a. immutable (never changing)

b. omnipresent (always with us)

c. omnipotent (all-powerful)

d. omniscient (all-knowing)

e. eternal

11. Write phrases from the following verses that describe Jesus as having these same attributes.

Isa.9:6

Matt. 18:20; 28:20

John 1:1-3; 3:13; 8:58; 16:30; 21:17

1 Cor. 1:24

Col. 1:15-17; 2:2

Heb. 1:3, 12; 13:8

Rev. 1:8

12. While Jesus emptied himself of some of His attributes when He came as a baby (see Phil. 2:5-8), God is love, and it was this attribute that we see clearly in Jesus. It is as though God is saying through Jesus, "Whatever else you know about Me, understand this: I love you; I want to be near you; I want to care for you." God's essence is His holy love for us, and this is what Jesus came to reveal.

One day an old gentleman asked God to show him a fresh proof of His love. God said to him, "Look at My dear Son hanging on the tree for you. I cannot give you any greater proof of love than that." What is the greatest act of love a person can give according to John 15:13?

Who Sees His Glory?

As we consider some to whom God gave a special revelation of himself, we notice that it is often in difficulties or
in crises God reveals His glory in a fresh way.

1. Moses was tending his father-in-law's sheep on the
far side of the desert. See Exod. 3:1. Moses didn't even
have his own flock. Plus, he was in a desert and on the far
side of that desert. How do you think he might have felt at
this point in his life?

2. Moses was far from the well-watered Promised
Land. What kinds of situations in life can make us feel utterly dry, as though we're in a desert land?

3. Yet, it was here that Moses came to Horeb, the
mountain of God (Exod. 3:1). *Horeb* means "desolate" and
is from a root meaning "to be parched through drought." It
is often in our dry, desolate times that we have a fresh vision of God, and we behold Him in a new way, a way we
could not have seen Him if all had been going well.

Have you ever experienced God's goodness in a new
way during a difficult time?

4. Moses was being faithful to the task he was given. If
he had failed to tend the sheep that day, think what he
would have missed! Often we see God's glory when we are

faithful in the mundane routine of life when all looks bleak. Why do you think God often especially rewards those who are faithful in the desolate desert times of life?

5. In Exod. 33:12-18, why is Moses longing for a fresh revelation of God?

6. God had given him the responsibility of leading his people into the Promised Land—a task he had probably dreamed of doing when he was tending his father-in-law's sheep in the desert. But now that the opportunity had come, he recognized the impossibility of his assignment. He knew God had called him, but the task appeared too big! "Show me your glory," he cried. Moses recognized that an enlarged understanding of God renews our strength.

Has God ever given you an assignment that was beyond your abilities? Did it cause you to look to Him and see His goodness in a fresh way?

7. Why would Moses not have experienced God's glory if he had felt capable of this role?

8. "In the year that King Uzziah died, I saw the Lord," wrote Isaiah (Isa. 6:1). Uzziah had been a good king and under his leadership Israel had grown in every way. See 2

Chron. 26:1-15. It is easy to focus our hopes on a significant person in our lives and feel forsaken when that one is removed.

When we feel abandoned by another, we need a fresh understanding of who God is. Read of Isaiah's insight into the invisible world in 6:1-6. Why would seeing the Lord as the Sovereign Ruler have perfectly fit Isaiah's needs?

9. Do you feel that you qualify for a new vision of God's glory? Have you encountered a desolate time, been given a new role for which you feel unqualified? Perhaps someone you looked to has failed you or stepped out of your life.

When Moses needed a renewed vision of God's glory, he asked God to reveal himself. Notice God wants us to know what to do to see His glory—to be aware of His presence. See Lev. 9:6.

10. Moses heard God calling him and responded, "Here I am." God knew where he was, yet Moses needed to respond to indicate he was listening.

How Can We Behold His Glory?

For those who have eyes of faith to see, "the whole earth is full of his glory" (Isa. 6:3). God wants to reveal His glorious goodness to us in every detail of life.

1. When we begin to doubt God's power, love, goodness, faithfulness—any of His marvelous attributes—we lose sight of His glorious presence in that situation. To the degree that we maintain faith that His goodness reigns in every detail of our lives, we behold His glory.

What was required for Martha to see God's glory? See John 11:40.

2. Why is faith required to see His glory?

3. God promised Moses that the Israelites would see His glory. How would He show it to them? See Exod. 14:4, 17-18.

Pharaoh had been the source of the Israelites' misery. See Exod. 5—11. Now God says He will show His glory through this one who had brought them great distress. It is often when we are faced with what looks like defeat and suffering that God says, "It is through this circumstance that I will show My glory. Trust Me. Believe that I will bring good to you through this difficulty." Those who believe His words see His glory.

4. Anselm said, "I believe in order that I may know."[4] According to 2 Cor. 4:4, what shuts out the light so that we cannot see the glory of Christ?

5. Before we can completely understand what God wishes to reveal to us, we must want to do His will. How did Jesus state this in John 7:17?

6. How do the following verses teach that willful disobedience hinders our ability to see our holy God?
Matt. 5:8

Heb. 12:14

7. Why do you think obedience is required to see the
glory of God? Consider John 14:21.

8. Pascal stated, "The things of this world must be
known in order to be loved, and Jesus Christ must be loved
in order to be known."[5] Would you agree?

The phrase "I . . . will . . . show myself" in John 14:21
uses a Greek word meaning "to shine forth," conveying the
same idea Isaiah used when he said, "Arise, shine, for your
light has come, and the glory of the LORD rises upon you"
(Isa. 60:1).

Glory is God's love manifesting itself.

Memorize: Oh, that we might know the LORD! Let us
press on to know him! Then he will respond to us as surely
as the arrival of dawn or the coming of rains in early
spring *(Hos. 6:3, NLT)*.

Prayer: *Dear Lord, beholding Your glory changes me! As
I behold the glory of the Lord, I am "being transformed into
the same image from glory to glory." How blessed I am, "for
the Spirit of glory and of God rests on [me]"!*

*Please give me grace to see Your glory—Your goodness
in every detail of my life. In Jesus' name I pray. Amen.*

(2 Cor. 3:18, NASB, and 1 Pet. 4:14 used in the prayer.)

Goodness is that attribute of God that
wills the happiness of all His creatures.

2

God Is Exuberant in His Goodness

ONE of the most tender names God used for himself was El Shaddai. The almightiness of God is expressed in El, a short form of Elohim, which means "the Mighty One." God was using vivid imagery by using this name, because Shaddai is derived from the word used in Scripture for a woman's breast. As the mother is the all-sufficient one to her baby, God is the Satisfier of His people.[1]

Shaddai suggests perfect supply and perfect comfort. It could be rendered, "God All-Sufficient." *El Shaddai* suggests sufficiency, bountifulness, perfect satisfaction—all combined with irresistible power!

Amazingly, Shaddai is most frequently used in the Book of Job. In difficult times, it may seem that God is far from being the One who pours forth blessings. But our faith rests upon the assurance that in the end we'll say with joy, "He has done everything well" (Mark 7:37). In every situation, He intends to pour out good on those who love Him.

Jesus: The Radiance of God's Glory

Jesus was in the boat with the disciples when they first encountered a storm (Matt. 8:24), but the second time they were "buffeted by the waves" (14:24) they were alone. Not until about three o'clock in the morning did Jesus appear to them walking on the water and saying, "Take courage! It is I. Don't be afraid" (v. 27).

Jesus allowed them to be alone in danger much as a loving mother bird thrusts her babies from the nest to teach them to use their wings. Jesus wanted to strengthen the disciples' faith so they would learn to be confident of His constant presence. In all their storms of temptation, He would be near. Even when they could not see Him, He would be an ever-present help in trouble. Sometimes it seems as though the Lord has forgotten us, but His eye is on us. At just the right time, we will discover He is with us and that His delay was indeed good.

Introduction

A recent E-mail brought a story reportedly told by Helen Roseveare, a missionary doctor in Africa. Despite her best efforts, a mother she attended in the labor ward died, leaving a tiny baby and a two-year-old daughter. To keep the premature baby warm, someone went to fill a hot water bottle. Unfortunately, the bottle broke and they had no other bottles. The following noon when Dr. Roseveare prayed with the orphanage children, she told them about the tiny baby also mentioning the hot water bottle and the sister crying because her mother had died.

Ten-year-old Ruth prayed, "Please, God, send us a water bottle. It'll be no good tomorrow, God, because the baby will be dead, so please send it this afternoon." While Dr. Roseveare gasped inwardly at the audacity of the prayer, Ruth added, "And would You please send a dolly for the little girl so she'll know You really love her?"

How could Dr. Roseveare honestly say, "Amen"? She had been in Africa for almost four years and had never received a parcel from home. She certainly had nowhere to go to buy these supplies.

At midafternoon, a car arrived at her front door and someone left a parcel. She sent for the children and excitement mounted as she lifted out brightly colored knitted jerseys, bandages, and a box of raisins. Then she felt the . . . could it really be? She pulled out a brand-new hot water bottle!

Ruth rushed forward, crying, "If God has sent the bottle, He must have sent the dolly too!" Rummaging to the bottom of the box, she pulled out a small, beautifully dressed doll. That parcel, packed by Dr. Roseveare's former Sunday School class, had been on the way for five months. Isaiah wrote, "Before they call I will answer" (65:24), and He does this more frequently than we realize.

If we could understand the goodness of God, we would never be anxious again. "The goodness of God" had seemed to Hannah Whitall Smith a vague statement until she began to consider that to be good is to do the best we know. Then she reasoned, "Since God is omniscient, He must know what is the best and highest good of all, and that therefore His goodness must necessarily be beyond question."[2]

At times the expression of God's goodness is limited, though, by our failing to receive the good He longs to give. Elaine Hardt described a dream in which she seemed to be in heaven surrounded by beautifully wrapped gifts. Jesus asked her which she wanted, and after examining them with pleasure, she asked Him to choose one for her. He placed in her hands a white tissue clad box. Inside was a breastplate of a high priest, and she knew the Lord was asking her to intercede for others. Even though it had been a dream, she accepted this encounter as a call to be an intercessor.

A month or so later, she recalled that unusual vision, and wondered aloud, "Who were the other gifts for?"

"They are all for you." The voice was unmistakable.

She could not believe it. After a long pause she boldly asked, "May I have them now?"

"Whenever you need to be reminded of My love or

need one of these gifts, just come and help yourself. All My good gifts are for you."[3]

I wonder how many gifts of grace God has for us that we will someday see were never claimed. He wrapped every conceivable spiritual blessing, and yet we often fail to see them because our eyes are not on God but on ourselves and our problems.

God Gives Generously

God is delighted to send us His good blessings. He is most delighted when He is most giving. In fact, He has greater pleasure in giving to us than we have in receiving.

1. The following verses all use the same Greek word, which means "good pleasure." According to the following verses, what does God have good pleasure in doing?

Luke 12:32

Eph. 1:5

Eph. 1:9

Phil. 2:13

2. What does He promise in Ps. 84:11?

3. God alone is permanently good. The words "He is good" were central to Old Testament worship. For instance, see 1 Chron. 16:34; 2 Chron. 5:13; 7:3; Ezra 3:11; Ps. 100:5; 106:1; 107:1; 118:1; 136:1; Jer. 33:11. What phrase consistently appeared in each verse?

4. Jesus would not allow the word *good* to be used of Him unless He was being recognized as God. See Matt. 19:17. Without God, we are utterly unable to consistently seek the happiness of another without regard for the pain it causes us. Only God is good in all He does.

How do the following statements teach the consistency of God's goodness? Which one means the most to you?

Ps. 119:68

Ps. 145:9

Rom. 8:28

5. Why is it important that we not doubt God's goodness?

6. How might our doubts about His goodness affect our relationship with others?

7. God's goodness provides a solid foundation for us. Good comes to us because He is good and so can do no wrong. He will never grow weary of doing us good.

Perhaps God telling Moses "I will cause all my goodness to pass in front of you" (Exod. 33:19) is what made Moses able to endure while seeing Him who is invisible (Heb. 11:27). He was able to remain faithful because He had seen God's goodness. Why does an awareness of God's goodness bring us into a more faithful relationship with Him?

8. God's words to Moses "I will be gracious to whom I will be gracious" (Exod. 33:19, NKJV) must not be thought of as an expression of God's capricious freedom to bless or not, but rather as an expression of the certainty of His grace. In this case the verse would read: "I am indeed the one who is gracious and merciful." William Dyrness states, "This is certainly no expression of God's arbitrary election as is sometimes thought—such a meaning makes little sense in the context—it is precisely the assurance of his mercy."[4]

The keynote in Ephesians is "Praise be to the God and Father of our Lord Jesus Christ, who has blessed us . . . with every spiritual blessing in Christ" (1:3). Paul didn't say God would give us spiritual blessings in the future but that they are already given.

What do you think Paul meant by "spiritual blessings"?

9. Every need our spirits have is met if we simply receive God's provision by faith. It is as though He has already placed every blessing we need under the Christmas

tree, wrapped with our names on it. God "calls things that are not as though they were" (Rom. 4:17). What did God tell Abraham before he had even one son? See Gen. 17:5.

10. What did God say to Joshua and his troops before they began fighting? See Josh. 10:8.

11. God does not allow His words to be of no effect. When He speaks His will, it is done, and the next time He speaks of it, it is as though it has happened. What God purposes to do is accomplished.

So when God says He has blessed us with every spiritual blessing, we know He has given us the rights to every spiritual blessing we need. "How great is your goodness, which you have stored up for those who fear you" (Ps. 31:19). The words "stored up" give the idea of a treasure-house where countless, unlimited treasures are held in reserve.

How did the psalmist speak of God's goodness in Ps. 145:9, 16?

12. In heaven, what good things do you think you may discover you failed to receive because you failed to ask Him for them?

Seeing His Goodness in Crises

My husband had a patient who, in the midst of extreme pain, saw God's goodness. Twenty years ago, Kathy (not her real name) was working alone as a volunteer in an art gallery, when a man came in, raped her, hit her in the head with a hammer (she still has dents in her head), and then began stabbing her with a knife.

During the attack, she began praying, "Our Father which art in heaven . . ." It made him so angry that he stabbed her just above the eye in an attempt to blind her. After stabbing her multiple times in her abdomen, he finally left.

"I don't know if you will believe this or not," she told my husband, "but while he was stabbing me, I saw Jesus. He had a crown of thorns on His head, and He said, 'I am with you. It will be all right.' I was lying there naked, being stabbed, but I wasn't afraid. I looked at His crown of thorns and thought, "I know how You felt," and I knew He understood how much I hurt."

The attacker thought he was leaving her for dead. Somehow Kathy managed to put on a smock and walked outside just as a policeman passed by. He called an ambulance, and she was taken to a hospital.

Before this traumatic event, Kathy had been reading about different religions in a search for truth. "But when I saw Jesus, I knew He was Truth," she declared. Beside her Bible on the bedside stand was a picture of Jesus with a crown of thorns.

In this horrible situation, Kathy found God's radiant presence to be infinitely more compelling than her pain. God's love, not the attacker or her suffering, became her focus.

Because God is good, we will always find that He is with us and understands and feels our pain. "In all their suffering he also suffered" (Isa. 63:9, NLT). Even when Satan intends to destroy us, God's presence is with us to bring comfort and understanding, and we can say with confidence, "God is good!"

Nine-year-old Darrell was burned so terribly that all of his body except his lips and one blistered cheek were wrapped in sterile gauze. When his seared flesh was touched, his screams could be heard far down the hospital corridor. One day another patient called out, "How can God do this to an innocent child?"

"Don't say anything against God!" Darrell's voice rang out. "When it hurts, God cries with me."[5]

1. Why do you think pain often allows us to see God's goodness more clearly than prosperity and good health?

2. God's presence does not always free us from pain and suffering. When Joseph was in prison, "The LORD was with him; he showed him kindness" (Gen. 39:21). Did the Lord's kindness mean that he was quickly released from prison? See Gen. 40:20-23.

3. Why do you think God's kindness to Joseph did not result in immediate deliverance? How did God's deliverance bring both more good to Joseph and glory to God? Joseph had been abused by his brothers, separated from his devoted father, falsely accused of immorality, and finally imprisoned. Then we hear him say, "But God intended it for good" (Gen. 50:20).

4. God intends everything He allows to ultimately bring us good. Because God is good, this statement—"But God intended it for good"—could apply to everything in our lives. As you look back, can you think of a difficult time about which you can now say, "But God intended it for good"?

5. Many times we cannot see God's goodness except through faith, but because we trust Him we know that He allows nothing except what He can use to bring good to us. As His children, we can say with confidence, "Surely goodness . . . will follow me all the days of my life" (Ps. 23:6).

Through faith we see the goodness of the Lord in circumstances that could appear to others as though we have been forsaken. The more we trust God's goodness, the more we will experience that goodness. The psalmist said, "I had fainted, unless I had believed to see the goodness of the LORD" (Ps. 27:13, KJV). Why does unbelief often prevent us from seeing God's goodness?

6. It is a comfort to know that God is working everything out in our lives in conformity with His will. What assurance does Eph. 1:11-12 give us in our disappointments and problems?

7. How will our knowledge that God is in control make our response to disappointments different from the response of those without faith?

8. Believing in the goodness of God transforms us in crisis even if we are not delivered. If in His tender compassion, infinite wisdom, and perfect love God sees that it is wise and good for us to suffer pain or loss or bereavement, should we not be willing to suffer gladly?

Testing may be God's way of leading us into a more fruitful life. A godly minister had an only child who was at the point of death.[6] The doctor informed him and his wife there was no hope their son would live. Their hearts rebelled against God and in their anguish cried out that God was unkind.

Then the Holy Spirit reminded them that God is love and gave them grace to accept whatever God allowed. The father said, "We must not let God take our child. We must give him." So kneeling at the bedside, they humbly gave back to God the child He had loaned them for a short time.

In a fresh way, the fragrance of Christ came into their lives! Every person in their congregation realized a wonderful glory in this fully surrendered couple. We, like Moses, may not know our faces (and our lives) are shining, but others will know and be blessed.

What change was there in Jeremiah's feelings when he began focusing on God's goodness rather than on his own affliction?

Lam. 3:17-26

9. Our learning to rest in God in a time of crisis can mean the difference between self-pity or the peace that comes to those who choose to believe God is good. Medi-

tating on God's mercy, goodness, and faithfulness will make it easier to trust Him.

What does God want to accomplish in us when He allows our sorrows and disappointments?

Rom. 5:3-5

2 Cor. 1:3-5

James 1:2-4

1 Pet. 1:6-7

10. Can we always assume that God's will is to change our unpleasant circumstances? Do you think Stephen's death brought greater glory to God than his deliverance would have? What did he pray for rather than for personal safety? See Acts 7:60.

After Stephen's death and perhaps in answer to his prayer, Paul was converted.

How wonderful when we can accept by faith these words:

> Good when He gives, supremely good.
>   No less when He denies.
> Afflictions from His sovereign hand
>   Are blessings in disguise.
>   —Anonymous

11. Why do you think the psalmist said it was good for him to have been afflicted? See Ps. 119:67, 71, and 75.

12. Rather than complain against God during a crisis, what should we do to bring deliverance, according to Ps. 50:14-15, 23?

Memorize: They shall abundantly utter the memory of thy great goodness, and shall sing of thy righteousness. The LORD is gracious, and full of compassion; slow to anger, and of great mercy. The LORD is good to all: and his tender mercies are over his works *(Ps. 145:7-9, KJV)*.

Prayer: *Dear Lord, I am hoping in You, in Your unfailing love; I am still confident of this: I will see Your goodness; You will provide all I need. My confidence is in You because Your eyes are on those who hope in Your unfailing love. Give me grace to see in even the most difficult circumstances that You are always good. In Jesus' name I pray. Amen.*

Just as a shepherd cares about each individual sheep, God cares about each of us. His love for the entire human race springs out of the high value He places upon each individual.

3

GOD IS ATTENTIVE TO DETAILS

Yahweh-Ro'i: The Lord Is My Shepherd

RO'EH (roe-EH) is a common word for "shepherd," and there is no more endearing term to describe the relationship between God and us. This name is used in that beautiful passage, "He shall feed his flock like a shepherd: he shall gather the lambs with his arm, and carry them in his bosom, and shall gently lead those that are with young" (Isa. 40:11, KJV).

Shepherding has not changed much in Palestine since the days when David wrote in Ps. 23, "The Lord is my shepherd" (my Yahweh is ro'i). A traveler to Israel wrote that the shepherd lives day and night with the sheep and establishes a degree of intimacy with them that is touching to observe. "He calls them all by their names, and they, knowing his voice, listen. He protects the sheep from thieves and preying animals that would devour them at night, by sleeping in the opening of the often make-shift sheepfold and they, sensing his watchfulness, fear no evil."[1]

Jesus: The Radiance of God's Glory

Great variations marked the different healings Jesus performed. Jesus healed one man in the crowd but led another out of the city. For one, His word brought a cure; for another, a touch brought healing; and a third He sent to wash in a pool. One received instantaneous restoration, but another first saw men as trees, walking. Before Jesus healed the deaf man in Mark 7:32, He took the man away from the multitude. Perhaps it was because He knew that the man might be more receptive in solitude.

His wisdom chose each detail carefully because He knew what would be the perfect way for Him to touch each life. We see His glory in His concern about the details of all that concerns us.

Introduction

It was a friend's birthday and she awakened at 5 A.M. A song began playing in her mind.

> There comes to my heart one sweet strain
> A glad and a joyous refrain,
> I sing it again and again
> Sweet peace, the gift of God's love.[2]

About two hours later as she was in solitude with the Lord, He told her, "That song was My gift to you."

How lovingly God watches over us! He knew that song would be the only gift she would receive that day.

Three weeks after her birthday she shared this precious word from the Lord by singing the song to me on the phone. I sensed that sweet peace, a deep calmness that was God's gift to her spirit, although she was experiencing great family difficulties.

Often we consider ourselves unworthy of receiving the Shepherd's best gifts. In this chapter we will reflect on how precious we are to Him.

He's Eager to Do Us Good

One of the defining aspects of love is the deep desire to give to the loved one. When we love, we find joy in imparting all that we have to make our loved one happy.

1. It is incredible that such an exalted Majesty should stoop so low as to admit us to His presence and give us a gracious hearing! Christ offers this note of assurance: "I say unto you, Ask, and it shall be given you" (Luke 11:9, KJV). He was saying, "I know the mind of the Father, and His delight in answering your prayer. Take My word for it. He will give you the greatest blessings He can give you." What promises does He give in Luke 11:2-13 and Matt. 7:11?

2. Christ tells us that our prayers are answered because of the Father's love for us. See John 16:26-27.

3. Often God opens His hands when we open our lips. What is the encouraging word in Isa. 65:24?

4. He is more liberal than we dare to request. Abraham asked for the life of Ishmael. What did God promise? See Gen. 17:18-20.

5. Isaac asked for one child. What did God give? See Gen. 25:21-23.

6. Jacob hoped for food and clothes. How much more did God give? See Gen. 28:20-22; 30:43.

7. Our Heavenly Father appears to be looking for excuses to do us good. It's amazing that He chooses to reward us so greatly for each effort we make for Him. If we resist a temptation, pray 30 minutes, give money to the poor, speak a kind word, read the Bible thoughtfully, or bear a little reproach for Jesus, He seems to be eager to reward us for it.

God loves us so much that He seems to invent excuses for blessing and rewarding us. According to the following verses, what are some of the things He rewards us for?

Prov. 25:21-22
Mal. 3:16-17
Matt. 5:11-12
Matt. 6:3-6, 17-18
Matt. 10:42
Luke 6:35
1 Cor. 3:8, 14
Heb. 10:35

God is delighted when our worship is in the form of service. In fact, one of the Greek words translated "worship" also means "to serve."

Have you considered that your smallest act of kindness is really worship and gives God cause for rejoicing over you and even for rewarding you?

Each Individual Is Uniquely Precious

With God, we never get lost in the crowd. We receive His loving attention as separately and tenderly as if we were the only one He had to care for. In all the religions Satan invented, personality is ignored, but not with our Heavenly Father.

G. D. Watson says in his book *Our Own God* that God could give an angel a description of our right thumb, or the particular way we weep or smile and without any other mark to tell us by, that angel could fly from heaven, and pick us out from millions of others.[3]

God also knows our secret thoughts, loves, and yearnings. He is the only One who can meet all the needs of our individual personalities. Christ loves us each so much that if you or I had been the only one who needed His atoning blood, He would have died just for us.

1. Write three phrases from Ps. 139:13-16 that indicate we are exceedingly precious to Him.

a.

b.

c.

2. God declares that you really are someone special to Him! Notice the different words God uses to describe our relationship with Him in the following verses. It is as though He wants us to know that He is the fulfillment of every relationship need we have.

Isa. 62:5

John 1:12-13

John 15:15

How significant does Eph. 2:10 suggest we are to God?

3. The Greek word for "workmanship" in Eph. 2:10 is *poiema,* and from this word the word *poem* is derived. You are God's poem, expressing His deepest thoughts and truths. Because we know that we are treasured by the living God, we can dare to disregard the idea that we are unimportant, that we are nobody. We are important to God.

What special description does God give to His people in Deut. 7:6-9?

4. The term *treasured possession,* used in both of these passages, refers to a priceless piece of jewelry—the kind in which a woman takes great delight. After a lady was divorced, she told a friend, "What I miss is being special to someone." God knows we have this need, and He repeatedly used the same Hebrew word to describe His people. See Deut. 14:2; Ps. 135:4; Mal. 3:17. What phrases mean the most to you?

5. "How precious are your thoughts about me, O God! They are innumerable!" (Ps. 139:17, NLT). God thought upon you from the beginning, continues to think upon you now, and will continue to think of you when time will be no more. God's notice of you doesn't consist of occasional bits of attention in a passing mood. He gives you His perpetual attention.

What do our continual thoughts about someone indicate about our feelings for them?

6. "Were I to count them [your thoughts about me], they would outnumber the grains of sand" (Ps. 139:18). There is a limit to the number of grains of sand, but not to the thoughts of God for you. You may at times be unimportant in your own sight, but never in the sight of the Almighty.

What did the psalmist pray in Ps. 17:8?

To keep as "the apple of the eye" (KJV) is an expression describing the most tender care. The apple of the eye is most carefully preserved. We are so near Him that it is as though our image is always in the great eye of God.

Perhaps the psalmist wrote that because He knew God had used that phrase to describe His care of Israel: "In a desert land he found him, in a barren and howling waste. He shielded him and cared for him; he guarded him as the apple of his eye" (Deut. 32:10).

It was in the place of the most horrible howling of wild beasts that the Lord surrounded His people. The Hebrew word for "guarded" means to surround with love and care, not merely to protect. Can you think of a time when you felt especially cared for by God?

7. If we're the apple of His eye . . .
   • He delights in us.
   • He wants us to spend time with Him.
   • He wants to comfort us in our failures.
What could you add to this list?

8. Write two sentences thanking Him for caring for you so deeply.

9. Dear Lord, You have said, "Blessed are all they that put their trust in him" (Ps. 2:12, KJV). In whatever area I learn to rest in You, I will be blessed in that area. I rest in You today regarding _____.

10. How do the following verses teach that God delights in us and we are of great value to Him?
   Ps. 35:27

   Ps. 68:19

He Is Interested in Us

Does God care about the little details of life? "Does God care whether we have pizza and salad today or if we have soup and a sandwich?" a friend asked while we ate lunch.

"God cares about us," I told her. "If we are greatly concerned about some detail, then He cares just because it is of concern to us."

"Oh, I see," she replied. "When my husband and I were on the cruise, I wanted to bring back a gift for my dad but I couldn't decide if I should get him a mug or a pen from the Cayman Islands. Now my husband doesn't care three Froot Loops what I get my dad, but when he saw it was such a big deal to me, he got involved. He cared because it was a big deal to me!"

1. When tempted to think, "This detail is too small to

bother God with," remember that He cares about what you care about simply because it is of concern to you. How did His miracle of turning the water into wine in John 2:1-11 show His tender concern with our human celebrations? Was the wine an actual need?

People would not have gone hungry or thirsty without it, but a bridal couple would have been embarrassed. How like Him to use His glory to prevent their humiliation! He, who would go hungry himself rather than ask the Father to turn stone into bread for Him personally, was eager to protect this couple from embarrassment. Doesn't it stir your heart to know He cares about everything that concerns you!

2. The word *friend* used in the following verses is *philos* and refers to someone who is dear to you, of whom you are fond. Notice Jesus' use of this word in Matt. 11:19.

3. In eternity the lost will discover they are lost from Someone who likes them and who wanted to be near them forever. They rejected the friendship of One who wanted to give them a place in His kingdom, the place of a bride. Being the bride means that there will be no closer beings to God in heaven. Pause and think on this awesome offer the Lover of our souls extends to all who will accept!

4. Tozer writes in *The Knowledge of the Holy,* "Many think of God as far-removed, gloomy and mightily displeased with everything, gazing down in a mood of fixed

apathy upon a world in which He has long ago lost interest; but this is to think erroneously."[4]

Other religions envision their gods as angry and petulant, always in need of appeasing. But think of this—we have a God who is singing over His people with joy! See Zeph. 3:17. Imagine what it would be like to hear God singing! Then imagine that He is singing over you!

For other verses that tell of God's delight in us, see Deut. 30:9-10 and Jer. 32:39-41.

Memorize: For the eyes of the Lord are on the righteous and his ears are attentive to their prayer (1 Pet. 3:12).

Prayer: *Dear Lord, You are the Lover of my soul, and I long to give You pleasure. I am eager to experience Your approval. Thank You for making beauty out of my failures when I confess them to You. I am in awe of Your love for me. In Jesus' name I pray. Amen.*

God always looks at a need with plans to meet that need. Our dilemma becomes His opportunity to do us good.

4

GOD IS THE GREAT PROVIDER

JEHOVAH-JIREH was the name Abraham gave to the place where the Lord provided a ram when he was offering his son as a sacrifice. It is a name we ascribe to God and means "The Lord will provide." It means God sees to everything beforehand. We never have a need that is not already met.

The key to discovering God to be our Jehovah-Jireh is to give up our Isaac, the thing that is dearest to us. When we willingly surrender our deepest desire, then, and only then, can we discover that God's provisions are always better than we would have thought to request.

Jesus: The Radiance of God's Glory

The story of Jesus' feeding of the 5,000, the only miracle recorded in all four Gospels (besides the Resurrection), gives lessons applicable to us in any kind of need. When the disciples saw the hungry multitudes, they appeared to be stressed, but not Jesus. The need did not frustrate Him. In fact, He already knew how He would meet that need. He still knows how to meet every need we have, but He also is still watching us, hoping that we will know He has it all under control.

Introduction

Nearly two years after *Women Alive!* magazine began in 1984, the bank account lacked about $200 to cover the printing bill. My husband and I were going out of town on Friday before the bill was due on the following Tuesday. After prayer, I was confident God would provide and fulfill His word in Isaiah: "Those who hope in me will not be disappointed" (49:23).

I went to the post office on Friday thinking, "God is probably going to have about 50 subscriptions in that box. Surely the money will be in the box today. God wouldn't be late with paying His bills." Nevertheless, I prayed, "Dear Lord, I give You praise whether there are enough checks there to pay our bill or not, because I know that down the road I'll be able to look back and say, 'Your answer was perfect! You did provide.'"

I went into the post office with high hopes. I opened the box and pulled out two ads, two changes of address, and two subscriptions. I walked back to the car, got in, and said aloud, "God, I'm disappointed." As soon as I said that, the joy of the Lord overwhelmed me, removing every concern about that bill.

That evening I remembered that Noreen, the circulation manager, had a checkbook, so I left the bill with her. One week later we returned, and I was curious. Had the money come in? I phoned Noreen who reported that on Tuesday someone had come to her home and written a check to *Women Alive!* that totally covered what was needed! Those who hope in the Lord will not be disappointed.

Preparing for God's Miraculous Provision

Let's consider Jesus' provision for 5,000 hungry people. The scriptures used are taken from Matt. 14:15-22; Mark 6:31-45; Luke 9:12-17; and John 6:5-13. "When Jesus looked up and saw a great crowd coming toward him, he said to Philip, 'Where shall we buy bread for these people to eat?'" (John 6:5). Jesus willingly assumes responsibility to meet our needs. His question, "Where shall we buy bread for these people to eat?" implied, "It is our responsibility to feed the people."

1. Jesus always looks at a need with plans to meet that need. Our dilemma becomes His opportunity to do us good. Can you think of a stressful situation you are in that God views as a chance to help you?

Jesus didn't ask this question to solicit information. He wanted to know what response Philip would give. He asked this only to test him, for He already had in mind what He was going to do. What was the test? Did Jesus really think Philip would anticipate a miracle? It's as though Jesus is always hoping for evidence that we expect Him to do the miraculous in our lives, that we anticipate that He will do exceedingly beyond all we can ask or think.

I think Jesus would have been so pleased if Philip had said, "Oh, Jesus, I know You can provide for these people. If God provided manna for the thousands of Israelites for 40 years, then providing one meal for 5,000 is no problem for You."

2. Perhaps Jesus was hoping for some indication that Philip would recall the miraculous feeding of the Israelites. See a similar incident in 2 Kings 4:43-44.

But Philip failed the test. "Eight months' wages would not buy enough bread for each one to have a bite!" (v. 7).

Perhaps Jesus had turned to Philip because Jesus had earlier seen evidence of faith in him. Philip had told Nathaniel, "We have found the one Moses wrote about in the Law, and about whom the prophets also wrote" (1:45). What faith was in those words!

When God tests us, He gives us grace to say, "Lord, I know You see that I have a desperate need. My small efforts appear to be a puny attempt to take care of this situation, but I am doing what I can. You will provide in the future as You have in the past."

One day, I repeatedly lifted a need to the Lord, and that evening, the Spirit impressed upon my spirit, "Have I ever failed you?" What a gentle reminder that He wants me to be confident of His care and to believe that He hears my prayer.

3. "The disciples came to him and said, 'This is a remote place, and it's already getting late. Send the crowds away, so they can go to the villages and buy themselves some food'" (Matt. 14:15).

"Jesus replied, 'They do not need to go away. You give them something to eat'" (v. 16). It is often those He allows to see a need that He uses to meet that need. What need is God allowing you to see?

4. What might He want you to do about it?

Philip answered Him, "Eight months' wages would not buy enough bread for each one to have a bite!"

5. Before receiving God's help, we need to acknowledge that we have no earthly way to solve our problem. R. C. Trench suggests that Jesus asked Philip this question early in the afternoon.[1] Jesus sometimes lets us ponder a situation to see how we'll respond. It is as though He is checking our level of faith. He knows the answer while

we're frantically trying to figure out what to do. Finally, we see we are totally inadequate to meet the need. Why is this an important step in trusting God?

Andrew speaks up: "Here's a boy with five small barley loaves and two small fish" (John 6:9). Andrew's emphasis is on "small." We see a need and we often feel totally inadequate. We say, "What will my puny efforts accomplish? The need is so great. How can my efforts to teach, speak, write, show concern, pray make a difference? I simply can't do the job that needs to be done!"

Jesus asked them to do something that allowed them to express the measure of faith they had. Jesus said, "Have the people sit down" (v. 10). They had to act as though they had food to give the people. Faith causes us to do what we would do if the miracle of God's provision had already occurred.

Jesus invites us to do our "tiny thing." In fact, His miracles don't happen until we do. He says, "Do you see a need? Do you see one small thing you could do to meet that need? Then surrender your supply. Have the people sit down. Do what you'd do if you had the supply on hand. Make ready for My abundance."

When a Chinese lady named Carol came from Taiwan, I had a mutual friend ask her, "Would you like to learn English by studying the Bible?" She responded that she would, so we made plans to meet on Thursdays.

The first Thursday we were to meet, I was still wondering what study book to use with Carol. That morning I attended our citywide prayer meeting, and in our prayer time, we divided into small groups. I sat amazed when the lady beside me told me that she was a former missionary to Taiwan who had been responsible for the printing of not only Bible study books with Chinese on one side and English on the other but the Bible as well. They were available for Carol and me to use!

I later shared this incident with Carol. "See how much God loves you!" I told her. This miraculous provision of the books was one of the things the Lord used to draw Carol to himself.

6. God wants us to go forward believing that He not only will see the need before we do but also will have provided the answer. What effort could you make to show God you are trusting Him for an immediate need?

7. Have you thought of some area of service? Is there a small step you could make to show God you are willing if He provides all that is needed?

Receiving God's Miraculous Provision

There was plenty of grass in that place, and the men sat down, about 5,000 of them. Jesus then took the loaves, gave thanks, and distributed to those who were seated as much as they wanted. He did the same with the fish.

Jesus gave thanks for God's provision before the evidence was seen. Perfect faith gives thanks before God supplies the abundance. His promise is as good as the deed!

Jesus was showing us that we are to give thanks before He blesses our efforts. We know He is going to provide, and we're so thankful! Have you ever given thanks before God supplied your need? If so, what were the results?

Before Jesus fed the 5,000, He took the loaves and offered them to His Father. How wonderful it is when He takes what we offer to Him! We can know that our gifts, talents, and desires are surrendered and are all to be used as He chooses. We pray, "Father, I recognize I don't have enough to provide the people what they need, but here are my efforts. Thank You that it is enough when I do what I can do. I give thanks because You love the people and will multiply my efforts to give them what they need."

1. Why might our failure to try to meet a need indicate either a lack of trust in God or a will that has not been surrendered?

2. Jesus knew His Father put it into His heart to provide for these people, so He was confident they would have all they needed. If God has helped us see a need, He is also willing to equip us to meet that need. Consider the promise in 2 Cor. 9:10-11.

"When they had all had enough to eat, he said to his disciples, 'Gather the pieces that are left over. Let nothing be wasted'" (John 6:12).

"Gather the pieces that are left over," He said as though tenderly chiding them, "Now see, you thought there wouldn't be enough." In Isa. 49:23, He promises that those who hope in Him will not be disappointed.

3. We often feel burned out and depleted when we've been giving out of our own meager resources. We do what we can with our five small barley loaves and two small fish and end up feeling totally inadequate, used, spent. Jesus

calls us to surrender our efforts to Him, to wait for Him to bless them, and then simply give what He gives to us. We will not be left feeling empty if we have given in His name. What is the promise in Prov. 11:25?

4. God wastes none of our efforts! Not one thing we do through Him will He allow to fall useless to the ground. How amazed the disciples must have been throughout that meal as they handed out bread and fish, their baskets never going empty. God had provided for everyone so generously. All ate until they were satisfied, and there were leftovers. How generous God is!

"So they gathered them and filled twelve baskets with the pieces of the five barley loaves left over by those who had eaten" (John 6:13).

Those who serve others receive more than they had before they served. The 12 baskets would have provided each disciple with a whole basket for himself. In God's economy, those who give to others find themselves with an abundance.

Do you recall a time when God rewarded you with an abundance in response to your giving to another?

Someday in heaven we'll see how God has provided all we've needed and we'll "revel in His love and grace."[2] Why wait until then? Today we can begin to give thanks for the loving provisions of our Jehovah-Jireh!

Memorize: Humble yourselves. . . . Casting the whole of your care [all your anxieties, all your worries, all your concerns, once and for all] on Him, for He cares for you affectionately and cares about you watchfully *(1 Pet. 5:6-7,* AMP.*).*

Prayer: *Dear Lord, You have promised to provide for me "superabundantly, far over and above all that we [dare] ask or think [infinitely beyond our highest prayers, desires, thoughts, hopes, or dreams]." Thank You for so richly providing all I need. Please give me grace to trust You to give me all that You already have planned for me. In Jesus' name I pray. Amen.*

(Eph. 3:20, AMP., used in the prayer.)

God's perfect faithfulness gives us courage
to approach His throne with confidence.

5

HIſ FAITHFULNEſſ ENDUREſ FOREVER

GOD is Emeth, the True One. Have you received a promise from God's Word that is yet unfulfilled? That word remains true. The passage of time does not detract one word from His promise. Repeatedly God assures us that He keeps His word. "God is not a man, that he should lie, nor a son of man, that he should change his mind. Does he speak and then not act? Does he promise and not fulfill?" (Num. 23:19).

Because David knew God to be Truth, with reverent insistence he prayed for the fulfillment of God's promise: "Let the promise you have made concerning your servant and his house be established forever. Do as you promised, so that . . . your name will be great forever" (1 Chron. 17:23-24). God, the True One, always keeps His promises.

Jesus: The Radiance of God's Glory

Sometimes it seems that God is ignoring our prayers. We might be tempted to think He is not keeping His promises. Could it be He has not noticed, or even worse, does not care that we are desperate for His help? When His help does arrive, though, we often realize that an earlier answer would have brought a smaller blessing.

Perhaps Mary was desperate for her Son to come to her rescue when it was evident the wine was about to be depleted and the wedding party was still going strong. He heard her request but did not respond in a way that assured her He would take care of her concern. Not until the wine was completely gone would the miracle be above suspicion. In Augustine's words, He might seem to have mingled elements rather than to have changed them.[1]

Only after all other help fails does our faithful Helper arrive. "Let us then approach the throne of grace with confidence, so that we may receive mercy and find grace to help us in our time of need" (Heb. 4:16). The Greek phrase translated as "in our time of need" means "in the nick of time."

Introduction

A lady in England read that when one prays for someone miles away something always happens at the other end. She had a brother in India who was not a Christian and she thought, "If I pray for him, will something happen? Is this statement true?"

She felt led to pray that he might come to Christ. Day after day she prayed and wondered, "Is something happening?" but in her heart began saying, "Something is happening; but I wish I knew!" After a few weeks, she wrote to her brother and asked, "Has anything unusual happened to you lately?"

He wrote in reply, "Yes, something has happened. Two months ago my thought was turned to God; I do not know why. It was not any book that I was reading; it was not any sermon that I heard; I did not go where I would hear sermons, but I do know that my thought was turned to think about God. I was led to give my heart to the Lord Jesus Christ, and as I write to you I am a Christian."

She checked the calendar and found that she had begun praying two months before. Something had happened at the other end.

One of the greatest surprises in heaven may be how consistently God answered prayer. Nearly 20 years ago, when my brother was a missionary in Papua New Guinea, he sent our mother a list of cities in which he hoped a church would be planted and suggested that she choose one for which she would pray. Mother chose Goroka and began to regularly pray for that city. Today Goroka has a large church with over 700 members.

God also answers precisely. In Exod. 33:13 Moses pled, "Teach me your ways." Ps. 103:7 states, "He made known his ways to Moses."

Later Moses prayed he would be permitted to enter into the Promised Land. God did not give him his heart's desire to go over into Canaan before he left this world. Still, God remembered his request. Fifteen centuries rolled by and Moses' desire was granted when he stepped into the Promised Land for the transfiguration of Jesus (Matt. 17:1-3).

"For the LORD is good and his love endures forever; his faithfulness continues through all generations" (Ps. 100:5).

God Never Changes

The great Shemah of the Jewish people is translated to read, "Hear, O Israel: The LORD our God, the LORD is one" (Deut. 6:4). One author tells of the Jews reading that line in their worship and shouting for minutes at a time: "One, One, One . . ."[2] Perhaps that means not only that our God is one God but also that God's essence is continually the same.

As humans, we tend to be "many." One day we're loving, the next judgmental, one time merciful, another time unforgiving. God is always infinitely loving, merciful, kind, just, faithful. He is never more just or less loving than He was the day He planned to give His Son to die for us. "Jesus Christ is the same yesterday and today and forever" (Heb. 13:8).

When David Livingstone was exploring in Africa, he was told that a savage chieftain with his band was surrounding their camp. That night, Livingstone wrote in his diary: "My plans for exploring this region and opening it up to the gospel are in question. Savage natives are approaching our camp. I am leaning on the promise: 'Lo, I am with you always, even unto the end of the world' (Matthew 28:20). That is the word of a Gentleman of the most strict and sacred honor. I know I can rely upon it." And he lie down and slept in peace, secure in that promise.[3]

1. God's changelessness is a dimension of His faithfulness. Read and record phrases from the following verses that speak of the unchangeableness of God.

Ps. 100:5
Ps. 102:27
Ps. 145:13
Mal. 3:6
James 1:17

2. Notice that the heathen gods were not considered to be faithful. See 1 Kings 18:27-29.

3. We consider the Rocky Mountains to be permanent and unmovable. How does God say His unchanging nature compares to mountains in Isa. 54:10?

4. How does God's unchangeableness compare to the earth and the heavens? See Heb. 1:10-13.

5. How will contemplating the unchangeableness of God bring us confidence that we can serve God acceptably?

6. When God says, "I the LORD change not" (Mal. 3:6), He does not mean He is static. Even though God never changes, He deals differently with us at different times. He only seems to change because we change and He must relate to us differently. In fact, we see a dimension of God's faithfulness when He changes His response to us. He will never punish the humble and repentant nor will He reward the proud and unrepentant. Can you think of other changeless qualities of God that may be perceived differently according to our actions? For example, see the first phrase of Heb. 1:9.

7. He changes His response to us to remain consistent. In 1 Sam. 15:11, the Lord through Samuel said, "It repenteth me that I have set up Saul to be king" (KJV). Why did He reject him as king over the Israelites? See verses 11 and 23.

8. Later in the same chapter, Samuel said, "He who is the Glory of Israel does not lie or change his mind; for he is

not a man, that he should change his mind" (v. 29).
Thomas Trevethan comments on this verse, "Here Samuel
is not contradicting his earlier words. Rather, he cautions
us not to see the Lord's repentance as identical to ours. The
repentance of the Holy One does not include remorse for
the way the Lord has been acting, as if he had done some
evil thing."[4]

9. Samuel is not suggesting that the Lord is surprised
by Saul's disobedience and must develop a contingency
plan. God never lacks foresight or knowledge or power to
carry out His plans. In fact, when it appears He is changing
His plans, He actually is carrying out plans made long ago.
Consider Ps. 33:11.

God changed His relationship with Saul so that He
himself would not change in His character or His plan for
His people. God knows our worst deed before we do it just
as thoroughly as after it's done, and He never changes His
love toward us. He is not waiting to lash out at us when we
fail. Instead, He invites us to draw near and find we have a
friend in the Holy One.

God Is Faithful to His Word

God receives glory, not because He makes promises,
but because we believe them and allow Him to show us
His faithfulness. There would be no glory if a mother said
to her child, "I will always be with you," because the fulfillment would be impossible. But when Jesus promises His
constant presence, He is glorified when we rest in the truth
that He is with us at all times. He is honored when we believe He is beside us when we're alone, and we're kept
from feeling lonely. He is pleased when we rest in the

knowledge that He is beside our children at school, and we trust Him to take care of them. If we acknowledge He is with us when we're trying to do something for Him, we discover He delights in our trust.

   1. Write Josh. 23:14 in your own words.

   2. Those who marched around Jericho dared, on the authority of God's word alone, to claim a promised victory when there were no signs of this victory being accomplished. See Josh. 6:5, 20; Heb. 11:30.

   3. God gave promises in the past tense. He spoke as if His promises were already fulfilled. See Josh. 6:2.

   4. In the Hebrew there is no special term for *promise*. *Promise* is simply *word*. God's word is His promise. It is also remarkable that the Hebrew term for *word* is related to the Hebrew term for *deed*. God's words are deeds.[5] With God no more is needed. He is so powerful, so unchangeable, that a word is enough. He speaks, and it is done. Once He gives you a promise, that promise is yours forever for that situation. What words of comfort or assurance has God given you? Those words will endure forever.

5. Circumstances of life may tempt us to doubt His promises, but not one word will fail. What words of assurance regarding His word are in 1 Kings 8:56 and Ps. 119:89?

6. "I did not tell the people of Israel to ask me for something I did not plan to give. I, the LORD, speak only what is true and right" (Isa. 45:19, NLT). When God enables us to pray until He gives us a promise, He intends for us to hold on to His word.

Find a promise in God's Word for your immediate need—a personal word from the Lord. For instance, read God's word in Phil. 4:19 concerning your material or spiritual needs.

7. If you're in a time of decision making, meditate on Pss. 16:11 or 32:8.

"Till heaven and earth pass, one jot or one tittle shall in no wise pass from the law, till all be fulfilled" (Matt. 5:18, KJV).

Behold His Faithfulness

Recently I read a prayer I had written over a year ago, and tears came to my eyes as I remembered specific answers to several of my requests. Satan wants us to forget answers to prayer, but writing prayers in a notebook ensures that we can recognize God's faithfulness.

1. What are other things we can do that will help us recall what He has done?

2. Why is it important to recall God's faithfulness in the past?

3. Why do you think it is sometimes easier to recall things other than God's goodness? For instance, notice what the Israelites recalled in Num. 11:4-5.

4. Before we see God's faithfulness to do the impossible, He often asks that we do our little part. In Num. 21:16 and Judg. 4:15-16, what was man's part and what was God's part?

5. Why do you think we often do not see God's faithfulness until we do our part?

If you do not see the faithfulness of God, be faithful anyway, especially in prayer. "To the faithful you show yourself faithful" (Ps. 18:25).

6. "Pray without ceasing" (1 Thess. 5:17, KJV) doesn't mean to pray without intermission; it means that we must not give up on our prayers. Often the secret of obtaining answers to prayer is regularly praying day in and day out when we feel like praying and when we don't. Apply Gal. 6:9 to this truth.

7. The moment we become determined to pray daily, Satan fills our path with distracting hindrances. Job responsibilities increase. The children demand more time. It seems we are more tired than usual. Satan suggests every possible reason for not praying. He tells us, "You are too busy; later you'll have more time. You don't feel like praying; God doesn't answer your prayers anyway." Before we know it, the entire day is gone, and we have not had time alone with Christ. We have a choice. We will either believe God's Word or we will believe Satan's whisper. When Satan tells us, "God doesn't answer your prayers," we might question why he tries so hard to keep us from praying.

How important is it to God that we remember His faithfulness to us according to Ps. 78:41-42?

8. Satan wants us to forget God's faithfulness, but God is delighted when we recall His works. See Ps. 105:5. Why do you think He is pleased with our remembering His faithfulness in the past?

Memorize: The Lord gave them rest on every side . . . Not one of all the LORD's good promises to the house of Israel failed; every one was fulfilled *(Josh. 21:44-45).*

Prayer: *Dear Lord, someday in heaven I will be saying, "Praise and glory and wisdom and thanks and honor and power and strength be to our God for ever and ever," and when I look back over every detail of my life, I will see Your faithfulness. I will see that You always provided all I needed in every situation. I will finally understand that You did not allow anything but what could bring good to me and glory to You. I will see reasons for praise in everything! Help me choose by faith the eternal perspective now and help me praise You for Your perfect faithfulness. In Jesus' name I pray. Amen.*

(Rev. 7:12 used in the prayer.)

Everything God does for us is done because He loves us. Love motivates every choice behind what He allows in our lives.

6

He Delights in Us

ONE of the titles God ascribes to himself is *husband*. "For your Maker is your husband—the LORD Almighty is his name" (Isa. 54:5). He delights in us as a groom delights in his bride! "As a bridegroom rejoices over his bride, so will your God rejoice over you" (62:5).

In Rev. 21, the Church is referred to as the bride, perhaps to signify the passionate love of newlyweds. Human love may fluctuate, but God's love for us never wavers. We do not fear God will forget us or the promises He has made to us, for we are His dearest possession.

God's pet name for His people was Hephzibah (Isa. 62:4), which means "My delight is in her." It still is today.

Jesus: The Radiance of God's Glory

Jesus "got up from the meal, took off his outer clothing, and wrapped a towel around his waist. After that, he poured water into a basin and began to wash his disciples' feet" (John 13:4-5).

To wash the feet of these men at this time was highly unusual, for it was not at the close of a journey when they usually brought water to wash away the dust of the highway. Nor was it a ceremonial washing before the meal. Why did Jesus do now what was usually done before a meal or after a journey?

He was eager for them to know "the full extent of his

69

love" (v. 1). His heart was consumed with a passion to express His love to these men. When He tied a towel around His waist, He was taking the attitude of a slave and showing His delight in attending them.

Introduction

While I stood outside an airport waiting for my ride, I saw a lady carrying a colorful bouquet of mixed flowers and thought, "She wants to greet someone she loves carrying a gift of flowers." The Holy Spirit seemed to impress upon me these thoughts: "That's how I want to come to you each moment. Each moment enjoy My love for you. Receive it, rest in it." God would say this to all who love Him: "Let My love be your joy. Delight in Me as I delight in you."

Linda Hardin attended a conference where a song was introduced that spoke of God's singing over us. It reminded her of this wonderful verse: "The LORD thy God in the midst of thee is mighty; . . . he will joy over thee with singing" (Zeph. 3:17, KJV). The words of the chorus "while You sing over me" intrigued her throughout the weekend. She continued to contemplate their meaning and imagery. She wrote, "I have experienced unfulfilled dreams; sometimes my path has been dark, and I can't seem to find my way. This song reminds me to listen until I hear God sing:

"How I love you, child! I love you!

How I love you, child! I love you!

How I love you!

"Sometimes I have run into the Father's waiting arms, like a child running to meet Father to share the news of the day. Other times, I have come carrying a heavy load. Then the Father gently picks me up, holds me close, and removes that load. Whether I run expectantly into His arms or come carrying my load, He continues to sing:

"How I love you, child! I love you!

How I love you, child! I love you!

How I love you!"[1]

What a good reminder that God is indeed singing over us. Contemplate how we feel about those we sing over.

God Takes Pleasure in Those He Loves

God's desire to impart His love to us is evident in what He created for us. John says that God's purpose in creation was His own pleasure. Could it be that God delights in and loves His creation because He made it for us, and we are His special pleasure? Don't you delight in doing something wonderful for someone you love? Much of the thrill of making something is often because we love the one for whom we're preparing it. A girl adds flowers and candles to the table for her fiancé because she loves him and enjoys seeing him pleased.

1. In light of this, how should it make us feel to notice God's pleasure in His handiwork as in Gen. 1:31 and Ps. 104:31?

2. What was the mood of heaven at the moment of creation? See Job 38:4-7.

John Piper comments on these verses in Job, "God does not say explicitly in this text that he himself shouted for joy. But do you suppose that God sat by with a blank face and no emotion, while millions of holy angels shouted for joy over his creation? Something would be very out of sync in heaven if that were true. I think God told Job about the joy of the sons of God because sons get their dispositions from their Father."[2]

Let's enjoy God's creation, seeing it as an expression of His love for us. Look at the beautiful mountains, flowers, clouds, and say, "Thank You, Lord, for loving me so much You created all this for me to enjoy!"

3. God is rich in love, and He lavishes it upon us—not just when we're deserving but continually. If we think He's going to hold us at arm's length when we've failed Him, we have the wrong idea. It's more like He's keenly disappointed. What does God delight in according to Ps. 147:11? In what way could you apply this verse and give Him delight today?

His Love Is Intense

1. God continually expresses His love in new ways. In fact, He has promised to never stop doing good to us. He constantly surrounds us with His favor as a shield, so that all that comes to us must come through His shield of love. What does Ps. 5:12 mean to you? Do you think we are usually aware of this shield? What difference does it make to be surrounded by His shield of love?

2. What phrases from the following verses do you find to be especially reassuring about God's tender care over our lives?

Ps. 23:1, 6
Ps. 34:9-10
Matt. 11:29-30
2 Cor. 9:8

3. When God moves He controls every detail. Nothing stands in His way. For instance, at the time of the Exodus

when the Israelites were to flee Egypt, God controlled the details they could not. Read Exod. 12:31-42 and record three things that indicated God was in control.

a.

b.

c.

4. Ps. 35:27 reads, "The LORD be exalted, who delights in the well-being of his servant." The *New Living Translation* states it, "Great is the LORD, who enjoys helping his servant." God's love has been described as His desire to impart himself and all good to us and to possess us for His own spiritual fellowship.[3] Using this definition, finish the following sentence. Insert your personal need and declare your confidence that God will control the details you cannot. "Because God loves me, _____."

5. God's love is compared to that of the intensity of the love a groom has for his bride. What does Eph. 5:25-30 say Jesus' love caused Him to do for His wife, the Church? How does this assure us of His help in our needs?

6. Twelfth century Bernard of Clairvaux described God's love like this: "In his very essence he is the Lovable

One, and he gives himself over, as the object of our love. He wants our love for him to result in our happiness. . . . Such generosity is there in the love he returns to us for our own. . . . To all who call upon him he is extravagant, for he is able to give nothing more valuable than himself. . . . With the refreshing of our souls he busies himself."[4]

Which of these phrases means the most to you?

Even When We've Failed

When God tenderly called to Adam, "Where are you?" (Gen. 3:9), I don't think He used the tone of a detective looking for a criminal. A. B. Simpson, in his commentary on Genesis, suggests His call is the cry of a father seeking his lost son.[5] God's coming to the Garden of Eden is presented so simply, almost as though He were coming to visit with Adam just as He had before the couple sinned. Of course, God was not ignorant of their sin, but His heart seems unwilling to believe evil of them. Perhaps He was hoping they would welcome His communion as before.

This picture of God's desire to have confidence in His people is beautiful. Later, we see God coming down to visit Sodom and Gomorrah to see if what they have done was as bad as the outcry that had reached Him. Then, almost as if He is hoping that the outcry had been wrong, He adds, "If not, I will know" (Gen. 18:21).

1. Hear the echo of His tender call to Adam and Eve in the story of the prodigal son (Luke 15:11-24) and in the shepherd's seeking his one lost sheep (vv. 4-7). Read these passages and record at least three evidences that they describe a love that was seeking to save, not to punish.

2. Notice that in Isa. 63:8, God's tone is that of a Father wanting to believe that His children had not turned from His love: "Surely they are my people, sons who will not be false to me." Does this picture of God fit with your idea of His response to you when you've failed? If not, how is it different?

3. God's eagerness to believe good about us and to seek us when we've failed has not changed. What is His call in Isa. 44:22 and 2 Cor. 5:20?

4. "O Israel, put your hope in the LORD, for with the LORD is unfailing love and with him is full redemption" (Ps. 130:7). The words *full redemption* are wonderfully reassuring. He can (and will) fully redeem any situation in which we have erred. All He asks is that we turn back to Him with faith and thoughtful obedience. His loving heart is fully prepared to give us a complete redemption!

Do you have a situation caused by your own failure in which you long for a full redemption? Write Ps. 130:7 in your own words, inserting your circumstances.

5. What is the promise in the next verse (v. 8) to all who need forgiveness?

6. Give Him thanks for knowing how to bring good out of all things. Reflect on the psalmist's words to God: "All things serve you" (Ps. 119:91). What are some of the "all things" we find it difficult to believe can serve His purposes?

Receive His Love

A little girl said to her mother after she had been disobedient, "Oh, Mother, I don't see how you can love such a mean little girl." Her mother replied, "You cannot understand. I don't love you for what you are, but for what I am. I am your mother, and I love you because of my mother-heart of love. I would love you just the same no matter what you did."

1. God set His love upon us simply because it is a law of love to love for love's sake only. All our fears and worries vanish when we discover the love God has for us. The first sentence of 1 John 4:16 says, "And so we know and rely on the love God has for us." The word *rely* means to have faith in or to trust. What role does faith have in receiving His love?

2. "God is love. Whoever lives in love lives in God, and God in him" (1 John 4:16). What do you think it means to live in love? Why is it equated with living in God?

3. The closer we get to Jesus, the more His love becomes a reality. Do you allow Him to love you? Andrew

Murray wrote, "The heavenly Father, who offers to meet us in the inner chamber has no other object than to fill our hearts with His love."[6] He invites us to make it our habit during our devotional times to let Him love us. What suggestions would you make if someone asked how to do this?

4. His love is not affected by our behavior. We may think, "I am so unlovable, God cannot possibly love me." How wrong we are! What might be some of the reasons we have so much difficulty believing God always loves us with perfect love?

5. Many people think they must create God's love by their own efforts. How could this mistake lead us into asceticism or legalism?

6. What do Rom. 5:7-8 and Jer. 31:3 say about our need to try to create love toward us in the heart of God?

7. As we learn to maintain a delighted awareness of His presence, what will be the natural results in our lives? How do we tend to treat others differently when we are confident of being loved and enjoyed?

8. Take time in silence to meditate on the wonderful revelation of God's love in Christ, until you are filled with the spirit of worship. As you pray, keep this assurance before you: "I am confident that my Heavenly Father longs to manifest His love to me."

9. How does this compare with the way we often approach time alone with God?

Memorize: I have loved you with an everlasting love; I have drawn you with loving-kindness *(Jer. 31:3).*

Prayer: *Dear Lord, teach me to come to my time alone with You as though I am coming to a lover, longing for Your nearness and wanting to enjoy Your fellowship. Even if my time is shorter than I would like, help me focus on loving You, wanting to hear You speak through Your Word.*

Heavenly Father, You've offered to meet me when I pray and to fill my heart with Your love. Because of this, when I begin to pray, let my main thought be of Your great love for me. In Jesus' name I pray. Amen.

God sorrows when we deliberately turn our back to Him even while, in His faithfulness, He is allowing us to suffer the consequences.

<u>7</u>

HIS JUSTICE IS GOOD

OUR GOD is a righteous Judge who distributes justice impartially. "Will not the Judge of all the earth do right?" (Gen. 18:25).

With God no innocent person can ever be condemned. Others may condemn us. Even a judge in a court of law may say we are guilty, but if we are innocent before God, there is no condemnation from God in this life nor when we stand at the Judgment in front of the Almighty.

Jesus: The Revelation of God's Glory

Jesus had just pronounced seven woes on the people of whom He said, "Everything they do is done for men to see" (Matt. 23:5). Then He looked over the city and with great sorrow exclaimed, "O Jerusalem, Jerusalem, you who kill the prophets and stone those sent to you, how often I have longed to gather your children together, as a hen gathers her chicks under her wings, but you were not willing" (v. 37).

Jesus had a passion for righteousness but an equal compassion for those who were unrighteous. His deepest passion was for His Father's will to be done, and He knew that ultimately those who did not obey would not escape.

Yet, if Jesus must pronounce a doom, He would do it with tears.

Introduction

Our guest arose from the kitchen table and stretching out his hands he began to quote Isa. 65: "Ready was I to answer men who never asked me, ready to be found by men who never sought me. I cried out, 'Here am I,' to folk who never called to me. I have stretched my hands, all day, to unruly rebels, who lead a life corrupt, pleasing themselves, a people who provoke me to my face continually" (vv. 1-3, MOFFATT).

He continued with tears. "I see Jesus stretching out His hands. What is He saying with hands outstretched? 'Come to me, all you who are weary and burdened, and I will give you rest.' At times I visualize Jesus above the street corners in Kansas City where orphans are being abused. I thought of Him when I was in India where there are 22,000,000 orphans. God is saying to them as He said to Jerusalem: 'How often I have longed to gather [you].' That's the kind of God we serve. He doesn't delight in sending people to hell."

How different this view is from that of those of other religions who say their gods don't care for people who have sinned. Our God is distressed when we are distressed. When our sins must receive the punishment, He is the one most deeply grieved.

When Adam sinned, God came to deal with him, not in that thundering voice we might expect from an enraged sovereign, but in a gentle examination. A child was reported missing in our city and a minister told of hearing on the news the mother calling for her daughter. In a heartbroken voice, the mother walked through the neighborhood calling with deep emotion: "Judy, Judy, Judy . . ."

He said, "As I heard her, I heard God calling Adam, Adam, Adam . . ." Surely the disappointment and sadness that must have been in God's voice drove guilt deep into Adam. We need to see a God who sorrows when we deliberately turn our back to Him even while, in His faithfulness, He is allowing us to suffer the consequences.

God's Law Is Good

1. One of the ways God ordered His goodness to us was to give us rules for living. He designed His laws to bring happiness to His people. This is the reason He wished that Israel would walk in His ways. What is His promise for obedience in Ps. 81:13-16?

Because God is good, He never asks anything of us that is not for our ultimate benefit. The purpose of the Law is to show us how to live to be supremely, eternally happy.

2. What are five reasons given in Ps. 145:8-9 that teach us that all God does, including the laws He gives, are ordered by love?

3. All God does is always for our good. How did He teach that in Deut. 10:12-13?

4. What phrases in Deut. 4:40 and 12:28 teach that He pleaded with the Israelites to obey His commands because it would benefit them?

5. God's laws are, as John Wesley termed them, "covered promises." What do you think Wesley meant by that term?

6. Which do you think seemed to grieve God more: the fact that His people had disregarded His authority and His laws were broken, or the fact that men had hurt their own chance for happiness? For instance, see Isa. 48:18.

7. He is said only to repent and grieve when men do not obey Him because He is then unable to give expressions of His goodness to them. How does this differ from many people's view of a law-giving God?

The Justice of God Is a Part of His Goodness

The rewards of obedience and the punishment of disobedience accomplish the same purpose. They both show how God values His own law. We prefer to think of God's generosity and ignore His holiness. "God is love" becomes our creed. Trevethan states, "A God who distributes warm fuzzies world without end is comforting, but in just the same way as pagan idols were comforting. They are a pale reflection of some of the truth, but mostly they are an exact representation of our inflated but fallen minds."[1]

God spoke of His justice when He told Moses He would make all His goodness pass before him, saying that He would by no means clear the guilty but visit the iniquity of the fathers upon the children (Exod. 34:7). It is a part of goodness to hate evil, and therefore, to punish it. It is no less righteous to give a person punishment for disobedience than it is to reward a person who obeys.

1. Why is it a part of God's goodness to make laws and attach consequences for disobeying the laws? Consider the reasons some parents do not make rules.

2. It is also part of His goodness to carry through on His warnings. A father who fails to punish his children is not considered to be a good father. Why is a ruler bad for his country if lawbreakers are not penalized?

3. God valued the Law as good when He made it. The goodness of God is based on wisdom, not weakness. Don't we consider it to be weakness to permit disobedience? If He allowed the Law to be disobeyed without punishment, what would be the results? Consider Eccles. 8:11.

4. "Justice and judgment are the habitation of thy throne" (Ps. 89:14, KJV). What does this verse say about the necessity of punishing the guilty?

It is His goodness that removes those things that would encourage us to depend upon something other than Him. One of the most loving things my husband did for my mother caused her much pain. Some friends had joined us for a steak dinner and suddenly mother left the table. Daniel noticed she didn't immediately return, so he followed her into the kitchen. He saw she was turning blue and realized some steak was caught in her throat. He knew this was life-threatening and immediately began the Heimlich maneuver as one of the guests dialed 911. Her fragile ribs were injured, but the steak was dislodged. Although she had sore ribs for a few days, she did not complain. What did sore ribs matter? She was alive!

If someone had looked through the window at that moment, they might have thought a lady was being abused. Often we can see only a sketchy view of what God is doing in our lives when we are experiencing what C. S. Lewis called a "severe mercy."

Just as a good physician injures ribs to prevent choking, God's infinite wisdom sees what is inconsistent with our happiness and in His goodness, He removes it.

5. How did the psalmist view His affliction in Ps. 119:71?

6. What might be an example of God's severe mercy in someone's life today?

God Is Eager to Avoid Punishing Us

God's prime intention in His Law was to encourage goodness so He could reward it. Because God is good, He placed consequences in His Law to prevent sin. Punishment is not His main intention. When His people disobeyed, He did not act contrary to His goodness, but against His first intention. He wanted to protect the people He loved from violence rather than punish them if they disobeyed.

1. God wishes He did not have to use severity. The Bible calls the act of His wrath His "strange work . . . his strange act" (Isa. 28:21, KJV). It was not His intention, and He appears to punish reluctantly. What does Lam. 3:33 say about God's reluctance to punish? Why do you think He is reluctant?

We also see His reluctance to punish in the way He delays punishment. He gives sinners time to repent, and He sends them messengers to persuade them to change so He can extend mercy. When He saw signs of repentance, He seemed to be delighted to forego the punishment. For instance, see Jon. 3:9-10.

Consider all God did to bring the Ninevites warnings. We tend to think the Book of Jonah is primarily a story of Jonah's encounter with a great fish. The bigger truth is the great lengths to which God would go to avoid having to punish the people. See the climatic last sentence in 4:11.

2. List three things God did to avoid punishing the wicked Ninevites.

a.

b.

c.

3. How does 2 Cor. 4:17 teach us that the judgments, hardships, or punishments God allows are filled with mercy and prepare us to receive great blessing?

In 1 Kings 21 Ahab tore his clothes in repentance. I think there was a tone of excitement and joy in God's voice when He said to Elijah, "Have you noticed how Ahab has humbled himself before me?" (v. 29). He was sharing exciting news much as we'd eagerly share with our spouse, "Did you notice how our child's attitude is totally changed? He's so much more obedient!" God delights in those who reverence Him. He is eager to avoid punishing us.

4. He wants His people to receive His blessing, not His punishment! How does Ezek. 22:30 state that God wishes for someone to appease His anger so that He would not strike the fatal blow?

5. How does God express His grief at seeing His people suffer even though it was for their sins? See Jer. 48:36.

6. Then it is almost as if He apologetically says, "I must punish you, but 'I will restore you to health and heal your wounds' [Jer. 30:17]." Also see His reassurances in the following verses.

Jer. 42:10-12

Joel 2:25

7. It seems God gave warnings, hoping the people would flee. See Jer. 49:30.

8. In her book *The Ten Commandments*, Dr. Laura Schlessinger says, "According to one Jewish tradition, after the Israelites had passed safely through the Red Sea and water crashed down killing the entire Egyptian army, angels began to sing the praises of God. But God silenced them, saying "my creatures are drowning and you are praising me?!?"[2]

In Exod. 32:10, God said to Moses when the people had made and worshipped a golden calf, "Let me alone" (KJV). Some think He said that, not so that Moses would not restrain Him, but because He wanted to give Moses a chance to pray for them. It was almost as a father who has discovered his child has disobeyed, but secretly wishes some friend would intercede for the child to repent. God longs for our repentance and is slow to punish.

Trevethan states, "God's generosity does not turn him into a weak grandparent, doting indulgently on our foibles, spoiling us with gifts when our lives cry out for discipline. . . . God does not wink at sin or tolerate it. God's goodness fundamentally involves an incompatibility with evil and sin."[3] The Old Testament speaks much of God's compassion. Despite the necessity for punishing, note that the following verses state that He is reluctant to judge.

Neh. 9:16-18
Pss. 103:8; 145:8
Joel 2:13
Jon. 4:2
Nah. 1:3

When sinners continue in sin, God's goodness becomes a threat. He then must punish sin in the unrepentant, to uphold His good law.

God's Judgment Is Preceded by Warning

1. Throughout the Old Testament we have the repeated pleadings of God and warning of judgment. See Jer. 29:17-19. Describe the feelings you think God might have had that caused Him to send repeated warnings.

2. Only after warning is persistently ignored and rejected does judgment come. For an example, what are God's poignant words in Ezek. 33:11?

3. The same theme of God's longing for repentance so He can avoid punishing continues in the New Testament. What did Jesus say as He wept over Jerusalem? See Matt. 23:37.

Also what is the clear word of Peter in 2 Pet. 3:9?

Jeremiah reminds us, "Because of the LORD's great love we are not consumed, for his compassions never fail" (Lam. 3:22).

Memorize: I will publish the name of the LORD: ascribe ye greatness unto our God. He is the Rock, his work is perfect: for all his ways are judgment: a God of truth and without iniquity, just and right is he *(Deut. 32:3-4)*.

Prayer: *Dear Lord, I praise You that You are not capricious; Your judgment is dependable. Everything You do is good. Help me to remember that it is Your goodness that snatches away those things that would encourage me to depend upon something other than You. Your infinite wisdom sees what is inconsistent with my happiness, and in Your goodness You remove it. Yet in all my distress, You, too, are distressed. I praise You for such great love. I ask this in Jesus' name. Amen.*

*God wants us to know He's our loving,
intimate Heavenly Father who assumes
responsibility for our every need.*

8

BEHOLD THE FATHER'S HEART

THE FIRST TIME God called himself Father was in Deut.
32:6: "Is he not your Father, your Creator, who made you
and formed you?" But an amazing statement is made in
Exod. 4. The Lord told Moses to tell Pharaoh, "This is what
the LORD says: Israel is my firstborn son, and I told you,
'Let my son go, so he may worship me.' But you refused to
let him go; so I will kill your firstborn son" (vv. 22-23).

God's message is clear: "It will be your son for My
son!" What an impact this truth must have made upon
Moses! God was calling himself his Father! In the New Testament, we are invited to call Him an even more endearing
term: "Abba, Father." Today, we'd say, "Daddy" or "Papa."
"How great is the love the Father has lavished on us, that
we should be called children of God! And that is what we
are!" (1 John 3:1).

Jesus: The Radiance of God's Glory

"Anyone who has seen me has seen the Father," Jesus
said to Philip (John 14:9). When we look at Jesus, we see
the heart of the Father, whose greatest concern is for the
welfare of His children. Jesus revealed the attitude of His
Father when He spoke of the shepherd who through suffer-

ing found his lost sheep. "Suppose one of you has a hundred sheep and loses one of them. Does he not leave the ninety-nine in the open country and go after the lost sheep until he finds it?" (Luke 15:4). The search of the lost sheep was the work of the Son. Although He was reticent to speak of His suffering, we know it involved incredible sorrow and suffering.

"But how does it end? With joy, and that was the joy that was set before Him, which made Him endure the Cross, despising the shame, the joy of finding that lost sheep, and bearing it on His shoulders back again. That is the Divine grace revealed in God the Son."[1]

Introduction

I heard a father tell about an incident that happened when his wife came home from the doctor with their young son. She said, "The doctor said David will need some special orthopedic shoes. Is it all right if I go buy them even though they are very expensive?"

"No," he said.

When his wife looked at him with surprise, he gently added, "I want to buy them myself."

That's a father's love, and Jesus was eager for us to know His Father as a Father who passionately cares about us and all our needs.

When Philip said to Jesus, "Show us the Father" (John 14:8), I believe he was expressing the deepest desire of the human heart: the desire to see God as Father. Perhaps He was saying, "Show us God as One who has the heart of a Father." Throughout the Old Testament, God had been revealed as the holy and almighty God and only rarely referred to as Father. Jesus, though, repeatedly called God "Father."

"If we knew the heart of our Father we would never question any of His dealings with us,"[2] stated Edward Dennett. Let's consider some of the evidences that God has the loving heart of a Father.

A Father Gives His Child a Sense of Belonging

When a couple in England signed up to be foster parents, they received training in how to treat the child. "Never make the child feel he belongs to you. The child belongs to the state and the state may at any time remove the child." When a boy was placed in their home, the couple sensed his need to know that he was accepted as part of their family and decided to disregard the advice they had received. One day the husband came home and found his wife distraught. The state had come for the child and they were forbidden to seek to find him. Nineteen years later they again connected with him and learned that some distant relative had come forward claiming they wanted the child. The young man told them, though, that he had always regarded them as his mom and dad.

Our Heavenly Father knows our need to belong and wants us to know that we belong to Him and assures us we "belong to Christ" (Mark 9:41).

1. What are some of the feelings and thoughts that result from never feeling that we belong?

2. Our Father gives these comforting words: "But now, this is what the LORD says—he who created you, O Jacob, he who formed you, O Israel: 'Fear not, for I have redeemed you; I have summoned you by name; you are mine'" (Isa. 43:1).

List two comforting thoughts from this verse.

3. We are thankful for God's justice, holiness, and omnipotence, but when we are heartbroken or have sinned, we do not run to His infinite justice, holiness, or power for comfort. We long for the arms of a loving Father who accepts us no matter what we do. God wants us to think of Him as a loving Father. See His comparison of himself to a father in Ps. 103:13-14.

4. How does He state in Ps. 27:10 that His love extends beyond that of an earthly father?

A Father Longs to Have Intimate Fellowship with His Child

The Early Church fathers discussed the question, "If Adam had not sinned, would Jesus still have come?" Some decided, "Yes, because He wanted to be near His people." God came down in the Garden of Eden and initiated close communion with His children, Adam and Eve.

This father-child intimacy is one of the great truths the Holy Spirit longs to reveal to us. Muslims would never pray "Our father," for they fear Allah would be terribly offended. Jesus, though, referred to our "Father" 15 times in the Sermon on the Mount.

Because of his work, a father had been separated from his son for many months. When he arrived home, his little boy was so delighted to him he ran into his arms crying. He put his arms around his daddy's neck and for a long time his dad quietly held him. Finally, the little fellow untwined his arms from his father's neck, kissed his father, and said, "Didn't we have a good time?" They had not said a word.

We need to come and worship, to tell Him the deep needs of our hearts. Sometimes, though, He just wants us to enjoy His presence.

1. Philip must have been impressed as he heard Jesus use the term *Father.* Jesus used it freely, not casually or flippantly, but intimately. Jesus invites us to call His Father "Our Father" (Matt. 6:9). John marveled at the great love in such an invitation. See 1 John 3:1.

2. When we as earthly parents choose someone to adopt, what does it say about our care for that person?

3. How much does our Heavenly Father love us, according to John 17:23?

4. We can't fully comprehend that God Almighty loves us like He loves His Son Jesus. God's Spirit is sent to our hearts to help us realize this intimacy into which we are invited. See Rom. 8:15; Gal. 4:6.

5. What does Jer. 3:19-20 teach about God's desire for us to call Him Father?

6. What should it mean to us to be able to call God our Father? Describe the type of intimacy you think God intends for this term of endearment to mean to us.

In his book *How to Pray,* R. A. Torrey invites us to visualize a loving Father when we pray: "We must have a definite and vivid realization that God is bending over us and listening as we pray. In much of our prayer there is really little thought of God. Our mind is taken up with the thought of what we need and not with the loving Father of whom we are seeking it. We should look to the Holy Spirit to lead us into the presence of God, and should not be hasty in words until He has brought us there."[3]

A Father Assumes Responsibility for His Child's Needs

"Since God called me to preach," wrote Rev. Lawrence Schaper, a minister who is now in heaven, "I never, from that day to this present time, asked Him to supply any of our needs. When I was a boy working for my father, He supplied all of my needs without my asking Him; now, since I have been working for my Heavenly Father I expected Him to supply all of our needs and He did. I believed God." Such an underlying confidence that our Heavenly Father will supply what we need both honors and pleases Him.

1. My father died when I was 15, but in those early years I don't ever remember having to coax him to buy me shoes that I needed or food when I was hungry. My earthly father knew I needed those things and happily provided them. What is our Heavenly Father's promise in Luke 11:13?

2. Notice the phrase, "How much more!" God is not merely as willing as an earthly father. No good parent will withhold from a child anything he or she needs, and God is much more eager to supply all our needs. What assurances do the following verses give regarding our Heavenly Father?

Matt. 6:6-8

Luke 12:27-30

3. "I will be a Father to you, and you will be my sons and daughters, says the Lord Almighty" (2 Cor. 6:18). The word *Almighty* means omnipotent or the "absolute and universal sovereign." What are some of the benefits of having such a Father?

4. How does Rom. 8:32 assure us that He will give to us on the basis of His infinite love and our need—not on what we deserve?

5. God invites us to come to Him with our every need and every sorrow as though we are children coming to our parents. What does the promise of the Father in Luke 12:32 mean to you personally?

6. Dr. Dennis Kinlaw stated that we get closer to the heart of God when we speak of His fatherhood than when we speak of His almightiness. Why do the words "your Father knows what you need" (Matt. 6:8) say a little more to us than simply "God knows what you need"?

A Good Father Punishes Those He Loves

We need a Heavenly Father who loves us enough to discipline us when we disobey. My husband recalls that when he was a boy, one of his best friends observed the discipline he received and wistfully commented, "I wish my parents loved me enough to make me mind."

1. What does Prov. 3:11-12 teach concerning the Lord's discipline?

2. God's hand of discipline is not that of a judge or a spiritual FBI but that of a Father. When my dad spanked me, I wasn't worried that he was about to kick me out of the family. I knew that he loved me too much. When God disciplines us, Satan wants us to believe that God is through with us and that He no longer wants us to call Him Father.

List at least three insights you find in Heb. 12:5-10 you find regarding God's disciplining us as His children.

a.

b.

c.

In disciplining us, God is doing all He can to equip us to be righteous even when we fail. He is standing beside us to help us.

In John 10:27, the original Greek could be translated to read, "My sheep are continually hearing my voice, and I am continually knowing them. They are continually following me; and no man can pluck them out of my Father's hand." Our Father will never allow us to be separated from Him as long as we have a desire to hear His voice and to know Him.

A Father Welcomes His Children Home

1. We need to see God as a Father who will welcome us home at the end of the day. Our Heavenly Father stands with arms open. Write three phrases from John 14:1-3 that speak of what the Father promises us.

   a.

   b.

   c.

"Mansions" (KJV) means rooms, dwelling places, abodes. We will go home to Father's house!

2. Why do you think He states in Rev. 22:12 that when He comes He will come bringing our rewards? What kind of effect does it have on a child for a parent to make such a statement to a child?

3. When we approach the end of this life, we know the Father will be waiting. His arms are open to welcome us home.

Memorize: As a father has compassion on his children, so the LORD has compassion on those who fear him *(Ps. 103:13).*

Prayer: *My Father, how great is the love You have lavished on me, that I should be called Your child! Give me grace to sense the wonder of calling You Abba, Father. Help me live each day remembering that I am loved and protected by my Almighty Father. In Jesus' name, I pray. Amen.*

God is able to do all that pleases Him,
but nothing pleases Him more than
using His power for His people.

9

His Aweſome Power Iſ for Uſ

THE FIRST VERSE of the Book of Genesis could be translated, "In the beginning Elohim created the heavens and the earth." Elohim means "the transcendent One." The Creator of the universe has all power. Nothing is impossible for Him except that which is contrary to His good pleasure. Jeremiah gives the scriptural definition: "Nothing is too hard for you" (32:17).

Elohim has absolute, unqualified, unlimited energy: the energy needed to make the universe. Astronomers estimate that there are probably 2 billion galaxies within 2 billion light-years of the sun. That is only as far as they can see with their instruments, and what is beyond that they do not know. "In the beginning Elohim," the One who has all power, said, "Let there be . . ." and it was so.

Jesus: The Radiance of God's Glory

When Jesus got into the disciples' boat to use it as His pulpit, He knew they had fished all night and caught nothing. See Luke 5:1-11. He must have delighted in knowing He would so richly repay them for the loan of their boat. He finished teaching and told Peter to go out into the deep and let down his nets for a catch.

Peter protested, "Master, we've worked hard all night and haven't caught anything. But because you say so, I will let down the nets" (Luke 5:5). Whatever we do in obedience, even though we cannot imagine how God could respond, He will reward abundantly.

Here we see the glory of the One of whom the psalmist wrote: "You made him ruler over the works of your hands; you put everything under his feet: all flocks and herds, and the beasts of the field, the birds of the air, and the fish of the sea, all that swim the paths of the seas" (Ps. 8:6-8).

An immense haul of fish is not necessarily a miracle. The miracle is in Jesus' foretelling what would happen. The timing and what it accomplished show us the glory of One who can use His power for us.

Introduction

In Sunday School while studying the awesome power of God, we read Job 26:7-14: "He spreads out the northern skies over empty space; he suspends the earth over nothing. He wraps up the waters in his clouds, yet the clouds do not burst under their weight. He covers the face of the full moon, spreading his clouds over it. He marks out the horizon on the face of the waters for a boundary between light and darkness. The pillars of the heavens quake, aghast at his rebuke. By his power he churned up the sea; by his wisdom he cut Rahab to pieces. By his breath the skies became fair; his hand pierced the gliding serpent." Then came the climax: "And these are but the outer fringe of his works."

"If these are the outer fringes of His works, what could be the center?" I asked the class more as a rhetorical question rather than expecting an answer. My mother-in-law quickly responded, "His heart." Her answer was profoundly true. At the center of His power is His heart of love for us. It is as though He tells us, "Oh, yes, I created the world and hung it on nothing, but at the center of My works is what I do for My people."

"I am not ashamed of the gospel, because it is the power of God for the salvation of everyone who believes" (Rom. 1:16). The gospel is the power of God! It is not the fringes of His works. Transforming and caring for His people is at the center of the work He most delights in doing.

Our God does not use His power to show us He can create worlds or try to impress or frighten us with His omnipotence as do heathen gods. He desires to use His power to bring us deliverance.

A Papua New Guinea national leader visiting in our home told us of a local tribe that for decades had been known as a warring people. One of their leaders heard the gospel. "That is what we need! That is what we have been wanting!" he exclaimed. They believed the gospel, and the character of the people totally changed. No longer are they a warring tribe. This is the ultimate use God makes of His power!

Let's first consider God's omnipotence and then look at His delight in using His power in our lives.

The Fringes of His Power

1. God's incomparable greatness exceeds our wildest imagination. He is above and beyond all we can conceive. Isa. 40 invites us to compare God with things we think of as great. "See, the Sovereign LORD comes with power, and his arm rules for him" (v. 10). What is the first thing we are told this sovereign Ruler does? Perhaps it is mentioned first because it is the work that is the closest to His heart. See verse 11.

2. What are some of the powerful phenomena named in verses 12-17? Compared to carrying us close to His heart, these are actually the fringes of His power.

3. Verses 18-20 describe a man-made god. How do verses 21-24 state that God's power is greater and His rule more permanent?

4. Creation is a witness to the omnipotency of God. "In the beginning God created the heavens and the earth" (Gen. 1:1). What aspects of nature do the following verses mention as being under His control?

Write at least one phrase from the following verses that shows God's complete and overwhelming sovereignty in all times.

Ps. 18:8-15

Ps. 107:25-29

Jer. 10:10-13

Jer. 32:37

Amos 4:13

Nah. 1:5

Hab. 3:3-15

5. How does Isa. 40:26 speak of God's power over the starry host?

6. "The heavens declare the glory of God; the skies proclaim the work of his hands" (Ps. 19:1). Our galaxy is made up of over 200 billion stars.[1] Scientists believe that the stars may equal or even surpass in number the grains of sand. Our omnipotent God made them for His own pleasure: "Thou art worthy, O Lord, to receive glory and honour and power: for thou hast created all things, and for thy pleasure they are and were created" (Rev. 4:11, KJV).

Why do you think it gave God pleasure to create? Could it have been because of His love for those who would be enjoying His created beauty?

7. The earth is whirling around the sun at 18.5 miles per second. Scientists have determined that it would take a steel bar 5,000 miles in diameter to resist the force of the earth's weight and the centrifugal force that would send it out of orbit. On what does God hang the earth according to Job 26:7?

Some years ago we had a pastor named R. E. Carroll who not only gave public lectures in astronomy but also challenged his congregation to see the glory of God revealed in the heavens. His teaching introduced us to the wonders of the galaxies and the incomprehensible size of the universe. The following description of the stars is taken from his book *High Conceptions of God:*

Locate Cappella, a very bright first-magnitude star, and just beside it you will see a small triangle of very dim stars. The star at the peak of that triangle is Epsilon Auriga. If you would diagram our earth as a ball one inch in diameter, you would have to diagram Epsilon Auriga as a ball four miles in diameter. Making that star was one of the lesser things Omnipotence did when He created the universe.

Our sun is 866,000 miles in diameter, or one hundred and nine earth diameters through. Yet Vega, another bright star is two and one half times greater than the sun. . . . Betelgeuse, a star easily located, is so large that its diameter is five hundred and forty times that of the sun. If our sun were at the center of Betelgeuse, then the planets Mercury, Venus, Earth and Mars would all rotate around the sun within the body of that one star.[2]

8. What do the following verses teach us about our great God and the stars?

Ps. 136:9

Ps. 147:4

Ps. 148:3

Jer. 31:35

9. "Consider the constellation of stars called Orion, always in its place in the heavens. Late at night one can see Orion with his belt marked by 3 bright stars across the waistline and the sword hanging down from his belt at an angle, marked by 3 more stars. In that middle star is a

galaxy. And in the middle of that galaxy is a hole. Across that hole, from side to side, there is enough room for 2000 solar systems the size of our solar system. Elohim made that wondrous creation."[3]

What did Job say about Orion in Job 9:7-9?

Consider the immensity of our universe. Although there are billions of stars, the universe is sparsely populated. "Put three grains of sand inside a vast cathedral, and the cathedral will be more closely packed with sand than space is with stars," stated English astronomer Sir James Jeans.[4]

His Power in Our Lives

Our response when we consider the magnificence of God's creation can be like the response of the psalmist when he thought about God's great works: "When I consider your heavens, the work of your fingers, the moon and the stars, which you have set in place, what is man that you are mindful of him, the son of man that you care for him?" (Ps. 8:3-4). We are, after all, the "inhabitants [that] are as grasshoppers" (Isa. 40:22, KJV).

1. Yet repeatedly we read of God's power, and then the passage seems to climax with a promise of His care for His people. He seems to tell us of His power merely to let us know it is available for our needs. He chooses to use His power for us! Notice this marvelous truth in the following passages.

His power described: Ps. 29:1-10.

His power used for us: Ps. 29:11.

His power described: Ps. 33:13-17.

His power used for us: Ps. 33:18-19.

His power described: Ps. 77:16-19.

His power used for us: Ps. 77:20.

2. God states His tender care of us in the context of and next to statements about His awesome power. It is as though He wants us to consider what difference He can make in our lives. He can do anything, and He chooses to use His power that spoke the universe into existence to care for us who hope in His mercy. Also see this concept in the following verses:

Ps. 65:5-6
Ps. 95:6-7
Ps. 121:2
Ps. 124:8

3. What is one aspect of His power mentioned in Ezek. 11:5? How is that power necessary to properly care for us? Why can God care for us better if He knows what is going through our mind?

4. Read Isa. 63:11-14, which speaks of God's glorious arm of power, and notice that it was at Moses' right hand to grasp him if he stumbled. What are some of the great things God did that are recorded in this passage?

5. Why did God divide the waters before them? See verses 12 and 14.

6. How does verse 14 describe the name God made for himself? What are some words you would use to describe such a God?

7. What does this say about how God wants to be known?

8. God divided the waters before them and led them through the depths. The depths in our lives represent the trials, the deep waters, the tough places we go through. It's easy to feel we'll lose our way when we're going through the valleys of life, but we can count on His help because He loves us so much that helping us is doing something for himself, His glorious name. He wants to be known as the One who uses His power to care for His people.

How does this compare with what people often do to make a name for themselves?

Scriptures abound in expressions that declare the infinite power of God. God revealed himself to Abraham saying, "I am the Almighty God; walk before me, and be thou perfect" (Gen. 17:1, KJV). It is as though He is saying, "Since I have all power, I can enable you to be perfect." He wants to use His power to perfect us. We will discuss how He does that in chapter 10.

9. How much is God able to do according to Eph. 3:20-21?

Memorize: Ah, Sovereign Lord, you have made the heavens and the earth by your great power and outstretched arm. Nothing is too hard for you. . . . O great and powerful God, whose name is the Lord Almighty, great are your purposes and mighty are your deeds (Jer. 32:17-19).

Prayer: *Praise be to you, O Lord, God of our father Israel, from everlasting to everlasting. Yours, O Lord, is the greatness and the power and the glory and the majesty and the splendor, for everything in heaven and earth is yours. Yours, O Lord, is the kingdom; you are exalted as head over all. Wealth and honor come from you; you are the ruler of all things. In your hands are strength and power to exalt and give strength to all. Now, our God, we give you thanks, and praise your glorious name. . . . Everything comes from you, and we have given you only what comes from your hand* (1 Chron. 29:10-14).

*God has chosen us to be what
people see when they look at Him!*

10

REFLECTING
HIS GLORY

Introduction

"WHAT is the chief end of man?" a Scottish minister asked a little girl. She was well instructed in the catechism and so replied, "To glorify God and enjoy Him for ever." The minister wondered how much she actually understood, so he asked her a second question: "And what is the chief end of God?" She quickly responded: "To glorify man and enjoy him forever."

Her answer was more correct than she could have known, because Isaiah reveals this amazing truth: God has chosen to adorn himself with His people![1] He wants the world to look at us and see His glory. "The LORD has redeemed Jacob, he displays his glory in Israel" (Isa. 44:23).

We who are called by His name are created for one purpose: to show God's glory to those who do not have the capacity to recognize Him. From God's first call to Abraham, we learn God had more in mind than just His own people when He said, "All nations on earth will be blessed through [Abraham]" (Gen. 18:18). God has designed that His blessing will come through us as others see His goodness and His glory in our lives.

We will first consider God's call to share His glory, to be His adornment. Next, we will learn how God equips us for this awesome role, and finally we will look at the results of showing His glory to the world.

Called to Display His Glory

The first book in this series, *Filled with His Glory,* discusses God's surprising desire for us to be His resting place, the place where He dwells as discussed in Ps. 132:8-14. It is equally amazing that God calls us to be His adornment: what others see of Him!

1. Although God will not share His glory with an idol (see Isa. 42:8 and 48:11), He is eager to share it with His people. Consider the following verses.

Isa. 43:7

Isa. 44:23

Isa. 60:21

"I, the LORD, have called you to demonstrate my righteousness" (Isa. 42:6, NLT).

2. Jesus prayed that we would be one with Him so we would share His glory. What did He say would be the result? See John 17:22-23.

3. Using the above thoughts, write a sentence summarizing the great purpose to which God has called us.

4. It is remarkable how many times God tells us that He made humans in His own image (see Gen. 1:26-27; 5:1; 9:6), until we remember that He created us "for the display of [His] splendor" (Isa. 60:21).

5. God's greatest beauty is His holiness. In fact, holiness is the only one of His attributes described with the word *beauty*. See 1 Chron. 16:29; Pss. 29:2 and 96:9, KJV. It is this moral splendor that He has chosen to be the adornment that others see of Him!

If God is holy and He made us to show His beauty, then God has designed us to be holy as well. In Eph. 4:24 Paul tells us that we are created to be like God in what way?

6. When God seeks to make us like himself, He begins by offering us pardon for our sins, but it is His purity, His holiness, that He most longs to give us. Hear His longing for a holy people in the following verses. Why do you think He repeated this longing so frequently?

Exod. 22:31
Lev. 11:44-45
Lev. 19:2; 20:26; 21:8
Matt. 5:48
1 Pet. 1:15-16

7. One of the reasons we are precious to God is that through us He will reach others as they view His holy character in us. "The nations will know that I am the LORD, declares the Sovereign LORD, when I show myself holy through you before their eyes" (Ezek. 36:23). Also see Ezek. 37:27-28 and Deut. 28:9-10.

Write at least two insights from these verses.

8. When He comes to dwell among us forever, it will be the beauty of holiness that others see! God's purpose remains the same: "You are . . . God's holy nation. . . . This is so you can show others the goodness of God" (1 Pet. 2:9, NLT). What spirit is necessary for us to reflect the goodness of God?

God is eager for His glory to be seen throughout the whole earth. See Hab. 2:14.

A missionary in India met the father of a boy in her school. "Have you ever read the Christian's Bible?" she asked.

"Oh, yes," he replied, indifferently.

"What do you think of Jesus?"

"Well, I think your religion is the same as ours," he replied. "We both believe in God, and we both believe that God became incarnate. Our god came down as Ram and Krishna: your God came down as Jesus. It is all the same."

"But are Ram and Krishna alive?" queried the missionary.

"No, they are not alive," he replied.

"But Jesus Christ is alive. He is living today."

The Hindu looked wistfully into her face, and quickly answered: "Show Him to me and I will believe."

This is exactly what God desires for us to do. A. B. Simpson gave the following illustration.[2] Sometimes an inventor will spend years perfecting some product to get it exactly the way he wants it. Then once the final detail is in place exactly as he envisioned it, it is comparatively easy to reproduce that pattern in millions of copies.

God desired to have a man with whom He could enjoy fellowship, who would delight in pleasing Him, and through whom He could show His glory to others. God scanned His best—Adam, Noah, Abraham, Moses, David, Solomon, and

Elijah—and, to His disappointment, saw that they all failed when tested.

God looked for a perfect man and found none—until He saw Jesus, the "Lamb that was slain from the creation of the world" (Rev. 13:8). When God saw Jesus standing on the banks of Jordan, He exclaimed: "This is my Son, whom I love; with him I am well pleased" (Matt. 3:17). At last He found a Man who met His expectation. Since that time, God's desire has been to reproduce the life of Christ within each of us.

That Hindu's desire will be fulfilled when God's people reflect His righteous character. We need to be able to say as Jesus said, "Anyone who has seen me has seen the Father" (John 14:9).

Our own efforts to be righteous are as "filthy rags" (Isa. 64:6), so how is His glory to be displayed through us?

God intends to have His glory reflected from His people, and He will do it in an amazing way.

Equipped to Display His Glory

For thousands of years, no one even considered the possibility of God's glory dwelling within humanity! It was awesome to the Israelites to simply have His visible presence in their midst. But God would not be satisfied until He had an intimacy with us that can only be compared to that of a husband and a wife. His Spirit would enter into our spirits!

The Son of God, Christ himself, can now be implanted within us, so that we can say with Paul: "Christ lives in me" (Gal. 2:20). Christ comes to live in us, bringing into our spirits the very nature of God. We can "participate in the divine nature and escape the corruption in the world caused by evil desires," according to Peter's amazing declaration in 2 Pet. 1:4.

1. How did Paul speak of the concept of God dwelling in Christ and in us in Col. 1:19, 27; and 2:9-10?

2. We hunger to be like Christ and pray, "Please, God, make me holy." With great joy, He responds, "I will come into you and give you My strength and My way of thinking." There is a problem, though. When Christ comes in, self must go out. For others to see Christ in us, Christ must be the one choosing our attitudes, actions, and habits. How does Paul describe this struggle to allow Christ to reign in Rom. 7:21-24?

3. What we need is to be transformed from a Jacob to an Israel. Jacob and Israel were two names for the same man. Jacob means "supplanter" or "schemer." A schemer tries to get what he or she wants at the expense of someone else. It implies the nature of one who is looking out for his or her own interests, the spirit of one who puts self first.

At a crisis in Jacob's life, God changed his name to Israel. The name Israel proclaims "May God rule."[3] God's name "El" is embedded in Israel, this new name that Jacob and his descendants would bear.

Notice which one displays God's glory: "The LORD has redeemed Jacob, he displays his glory in Israel" (Isa. 44:23). How wonderful to be Jacob, the redeemed! But it is through Israel that God displays His glory. Why must "May God rule" describe our nature before God can display His splendor through us?

4. We rejoice that we are redeemed as Jacob was. Our sins are covered by Jesus' blood, so God does not see them. But God is concerned about the people who do see our sins. He wants to reveal himself to them through us. Name three attitudes others see when our nature is that of Israel—"May God rule."

5. Read about Jacob's life-changing encounter in Gen. 32 and write the phrases from the verses that speak of the things that had to occur before Jacob became Israel.

a. Jacob wanted to surrender, but it was a struggle. Our selfish nature does not give up control easily. Only with supernatural help can self be overcome. Jacob was determined to wait for the blessing. Perseverance is an important step in faith.

b. Jacob had to be honest about his carnal tendency to want self to rule.

6. After Jacob became Israel, he no longer walked with proud strides. How do you think seeing his brother with a hesitant limp might have affected Esau? Read Gen. 33:1-3. How does the humble spirit of a fully surrendered life similarly affect others?

When those with whom we have a conflict can observe nothing in us except a spirit that wants to please God, they see the glory of His presence.

According to *The Torah: A Modern Commentary,* the conquest of the Promised Land started at the place where Jacob wrestled with the angel (Num. 21:24).[4] We, too, enter the Promised Land of rest when we receive an inner longing that says, "May God rule."

7. Many seek to surrender as Jacob did but still do not experience the pure joy of being able to say with certainty, "I have been crucified with Christ and I no longer live, but Christ lives in me" (Gal. 2:20). Instead, they admit, "I have the desire to do what is good, but I cannot carry it out" (Rom. 7:18).

They are like the 10 spies who failed to believe it would be possible to live in Canaan, the land of rest. See Num. 13. Why did the Israelites not enter their Promised Land, according to Heb. 3:19?

8. Canaan represents the spiritual land where we have rest from the selfish nature within because God has given us undivided hearts. What did He promise in Jer. 32:39 and Ezek. 11:19; 36:25-27?

9. If you have trusted the Lord for pardon for your sins, you are redeemed. That is cause for rejoicing! But have you also trusted Him for purity? What role does faith play in our being purified so Christ can indwell us, giving us an individed heart? See Acts 15:9 and Gal. 3:14.

When we take a breath, we don't wonder if the air will come in. God wants us to be equally confident that His Spirit will purify our hearts when we fully surrender to Him.

10. In 1870, Caroline Noel wrote:
In your hearts enthrone Him; There let Him remove
All that is not holy, All that is not true.[5]

When we trust Him to remove all that is not holy, God's Spirit comes in as a refining fire. With a cleansed, undivided heart, we have power in every situation to say, "May God rule!" Christ enthroned within gives us His desire: "I desire to do your will, O my God; your law is within my heart" (Ps. 40:8). When His law is within our hearts, it's as natural for us to want to obey God as it is for the birds to fly.

A desire to give God glory becomes the passion of our lives just as it was the passion of Christ.

Displaying His Glory

1. "Awake, awake, O Zion, clothe yourself with strength" (Isa. 52:1). Zion refers to the Church,[6] and Isaiah is calling the Church to embrace the glory that is hers in God. Compare this to Luke 24:49.

2. What did the coming of the Holy Spirit equip the disciples to do? See Acts 1:8.

3. The Holy Spirit fills those who are willing to say, "May God rule!" When our spirits are characterized by the

rule of Christ, others will sense a difference about us. When the nurses came into the hospital room of my friend's Christian mother, they would say, "There is something different about that room." A nurse told me that sometimes patients have said for no reason that she could determine, "You're a Christian, aren't you?"

When God called Moses to lead the Israelites, Moses prayed, "What else will distinguish me and your people from all the other people on the face of the earth?" (Exod. 33:16). We are indeed to be different, but in what way? For what was Moses pleading? See verses 15-16.

4. The glory of His presence is still the distinguishing mark of God's people! If God's presence is not with us, we have nothing to mark us as distinct from anyone else. What are some of the things people sometimes believe identify them as God's people rather than His presence? Do those things show God's glory, His love and tender concern for others?

5. God is Spirit and He will reveal His Spirit through our spirit. When our spirit is the same as that of the Spirit of Christ, others will sense the presence of God. What should characterize the spirit of those who reflect a holy God? See Gal. 5:22-23.

6. Read through the headings of chapters 2 through 9. Consider ways you can allow these aspects of His glory to be seen through you. Write down any ideas the Spirit brings to your mind.

When you are with non-Christians, see yourself as God sees you. Perhaps He is saying, "She is showing them what I'm like. Others are discovering My delight in them, My desire to attend to their needs! How wonderful that they are learning that I love them and that I delight in making My resources available for their needs."

No wonder God says, "Whoever touches you touches the apple of [My] eye" (Zech. 2:8). It is through us that the knowledge of the glory of God fills the earth.

Memorize: Arise, shine, for your light has come, and the glory of the LORD rises upon you *(Isa. 60:1)*.

Prayer: *Dear Lord, You have given me the incredible offer of being Your adornment, Your beauty that others see. You offer to give Me yourself as intimately as a husband gives himself to his wife.*

I have no greater thrill than totally surrendering to You! In return, You give me Your own Spirit through whom I am enabled to show Your love to others.

May Your promise, "I will fill this house with glory" (Hag. 2:7), be fulfilled in me. In Jesus' name I will praise You forever. Amen.

Appendix

Suggestions for Leaders

The importance of a name to the biblical writers cannot be overstated. They noted that God knew Moses by name (Exod. 33:17) and called Cyrus by name (Isa. 45:1-3). They filled whole pages with names. See Gen. 5; Num. 1—3; Matt. 1:1-17; Luke 3:23-38. Quietly, but emphatically, they tell us that our names are significant to God. He tells us, "I have summoned you by name; you are mine" (Isa. 43:1).

You may want to discuss the importance of names in making us human: a being that forms a relationship. For instance, parents begin to consider a name for their child as soon as they know they are to be parents. How does God naming himself and calling us by name teach us of His desire for a relationship with Him?

The questions in this study are of two types. One type asks that you look up and record what Scripture says. This is not to be done merely as an exercise. The student should be a listener who wants to better understand. The Hebrew word for "manna" means "what is it?" because those words sound like what the Israelites said when they saw the manna on the ground. Before God's Word can become manna to us, we, too, must ask, "What is it?" "What is it to me?" "What does it mean for my life?" Then, when we are eager to know, God gives us understanding, and His Word becomes bread for our spirits.

The second type of question aims to help you make application of truth, to assist you in changing the material into the spiritual, so Christ can be formed in your life. Participation should be optional for all questions, but especially those that require a personal response.

Be willing to share what the Holy Spirit teaches you. Samuel Logan Brengle, one of the great leaders of the Salvation Army, believed in sharing his own personal experience. "I look upon God's dealings with my soul, not as something to be hidden in my own heart for my personal comfort and guidance, but as a trust for the tempted and hungry-hearted who will hear and read me."[1] God will make you a channel of His blessings as you share His work in your life.

Additional Chapter Comments

Chapter 1

The Son revealed God's glory throughout His life. An amazing number of references associating Him with glory or light are in the New Testament. For instance, at Jesus' birth, the shepherds saw the glory of the Lord in Luke 2:9. His glory was especially transparent on the Mount of Transfiguration in Luke 9:29 and 2 Pet. 1:16-18. Shortly before His death, Jesus stated in His prayer that the Son shares in the glory of the Father and prayed that believers may also share in this glory. See John 17:22.

The association of Jesus with the Shechinah is also apparent in the Epistles. Paul saw the glory of the resurrected Jesus and was blinded by His brightness (Acts 9:3-9; 22:6-11; 26:11-18). Paul used the concept of dwelling (Shechinah) to teach the mystery of the Incarnation (the dwelling of God in human flesh). See Col. 1:19; 2:9. Perhaps you will find others as you begin to notice these references.

Chapter 2

According to Paul, one day God is going to have an exhibit. All of His goodness to us will be on display. "God raised us up with Christ and seated us with him in the heavenly realms in Christ Jesus, in order that in the coming ages he might show the incomparable riches of his grace, expressed in his kindness to us in Christ Jesus" (Eph. 2:6-7). Paul is saying this, "All through eternity God wants the riches of His grace, expressed through His kindness to us, to be on display. All eternity His works in our lives will be exhibited. His goodness to us will bring Him glory forever!"

Details on displays are important. After painting our bedroom walls, we saw a nail hole and my husband filled it with toothpaste suggesting that I cover the white spot with paint. Before I did that, my friend Sharon came over, and I invited her to see the new painting we had hung above our bed. I noticed that despite the new picture, her eyes went to that dot of white toothpaste.

I think of that when I read of the presentation of kindness God intends to make throughout eternity. He is not going to have one tiny flaw. A single failure to do us good would ruin His display. There will not be one time about which we will be able to say, "God, that detail, that pain You allowed in my life was not good."

The goodness of God appears differently to different people. One man said, "The fact that God can make all things work together for good, even the mess I make of things, that is God's glory to me!" What do those in your class see as God's goodness to them?

Chapter 3

We once had a column in the *Women Alive!* magazine called "Evidences of God's Love" and invited women to write us, telling what they consider to be evidences of divine love in their lives. Their responses were nearly all specific needs God supplied, many of them seemingly very trivial and often more a desire than a true need. They included:

- a ride home after a car stalled
- apples for an apple pie
- a sewing machine for a relative
- some new blazers

God shows us His love by attending to the details in our lives. You might give opportunity for the class to discuss evidences of God's loving concern shown in all ways to them. Do they think people were more aware of God's love during the depression when they needed to trust Him for many desperate needs? "The Lord takes thought and plans for me" (Ps. 40:17, AMP.). Do we nurture our intimate love relationship with God, or do we take His infinite concern for us for granted? What are some special ways we can express our gratitude to Him?

Chapter 4

Sometimes we think we need to be "worthy" to receive God's blessings. But we can learn from Jesus' attitude to the crowd. Before He fed the multitudes He did not ask them about their behavior. We can be sure that a gathering of 5,000 men plus women and children included a strange assortment, but He wanted all to receive His blessing. He fed them a meal just as they were. All they needed to qualify for His bread and fish was to be hungry. Those who hunger always touch the heart of God. It was as though Jesus said to the crowd, "I love and pity you so much that I will feed and care for you even though you are going to crucify Me." No doubt there were some in that crowd who responded to that meal offered to them in love and found a hunger in their spirits for the true Bread.

Chapter 5

After the miraculous feeding of the 5,000, the disciples got into their boat and encountered a storm. Jesus went to them and when the disciples saw Him walking on the lake, they were terrified. Why would the disciples be terrified, having just encountered Jesus' miraculous power to provide all that they needed?

Yet isn't it always that way in times of difficulty and distress? Our minds seem to delete all memory of God's mighty deliverances of the past when we are in a new difficulty. God divided the Red Sea, but when the Israelites met a new trouble they cried, "Is the LORD among us or not?" (Exod. 17:7; see vv. 1-7). Only those with a mature faith who look to God's former dealings of faithfulness and love are confident He will provide in the future as He has in the past.

Contrast the disciples with David, who chose to believe God in a new situation because he had learned from

God's faithfulness in the past. "But David said to Saul, 'Your servant has been keeping his father's sheep. When a lion or a bear came and carried off a sheep from the flock, I went after it, struck it and rescued the sheep from its mouth. When it turned on me, I seized it by its hair, struck it and killed it. Your servant has killed both the lion and the bear; this uncircumcised Philistine will be like one of them, because he has defied the armies of the living God. The LORD who delivered me from the paw of the lion and the paw of the bear will deliver me from the hand of this Philistine.' Saul said to David, 'Go, and the LORD be with you'" (1 Sam. 17:34-37). Another example is given in 2 Chron. 16:7-8.

Chapter 6

In Eph. 3:18, Paul prayed that the Ephesians would "have power, together with all the saints, to grasp how wide and long and high and deep is the love of Christ." Consider each of these dimensions and see if you can think of applications in your own life: both of how God loves you and of how you can allow His love to be poured through your heart to others.

How wide is the love of Christ? His love reaches to all areas of our lives, to all classes of society. His love is wide enough to reach us even when we've failed.

How long is the love of Christ? His love is forever. Our love may wear thin; we may wonder, "How long, O Lord, how long will I have to put up with this condition? This bad relationship? This person who has failed?" God says, "If your love reflects Mine, your love will endure forever."

How high is the love of Christ? What's the highest kind of love you can think of? God's love is higher. See Rom. 5:6-8.

How deep is the love of Christ? When we're in the depths of despair, when we've fallen flat on our faces, God's love is still beneath us.

Chapter 7

Jesus had a kind spirit toward those who others wanted to condemn. "'Master,' said John, 'we saw a man driving out demons in your name and we tried to stop him, because he was not one of us.' 'Do not stop him, . . . for whoever is not against you is for you'" (Luke 9:49).

Then in Luke 9:54 when Jesus was not welcomed by people because He was headed for Jerusalem, the disciples said, "'Do you want us to call fire down from heaven to destroy them?' But Jesus turned and rebuked them."

Now it often seems that evil prevails. But one day all evil will meet its final doom. When two demon-possessed men asked Jesus, "Have you come here to torture us before the appointed time?" (Matt. 8:29), by the demons' own confession, a time is coming when Jesus shall be Victor over all evil. No evil will then be allowed to go unpunished.

Chapter 8

Once we have entered into God's family, we gain immediate "access to the Father's lap. . . . The problem is: either we don't know it; we know it but we don't accept it; we accept it but are not in touch with it; we are in touch with it but do not surrender to it."[1]

Before the world began, God chose to call us not servants, but sons and daughters. "He predestined us to be adopted as his sons through Jesus Christ, in accordance with his pleasure and will" (Eph. 1:5). "I will be a Father to you, and you will be my sons and daughters, says the Lord Almighty" (2 Cor. 6:18).

God was especially concerned about those who had no earthly father and gave them special assurances of His parental care. "A father to the fatherless, a defender of widows, is God in his holy dwelling" (Ps. 68:5).

Chapter 9

God knows all things. He does not simply have the

power or ability to know—but He does know. Every minute detail of the past and future are seen with as much clearness as the present. In one intuitive glance, He can see the most loving way to answer your prayer. His answer will be good in all ways and will respond to every ounce of faith.

"Ponder anew what the Almighty can do,

If with His love He befriend thee."[2]

From antiquity there have been constellations in the skies that we call the Cross, the Crown, the Serpent, the Conquering Hero, the Lion, and the Virgin. An unverified report states that before the birth of Christ, a star, believed to be the star that signified the coming of Christ, moved toward the constellation of the Virgin. Now that same star is moving in the direction of the Lion, the sign of royalty and of powerful rule.[3]

Notice how responsive the earth is to the power of God.

- His storm expressed His power (Ps. 29:3-9).
- Good weather indicated His favor (Ps. 107:25-29).
- God is the rider of clouds (Ps. 68:4).
- He is Lord of the earthquake (Nah. 1:5).
- Earthquakes, clouds, lightning, darkness, and thunder accompany His appearances (Pss. 18:8-16; 68:7-9; Hab. 3:3-15).
- But it is in the deliverance of His people that His wrath and His goodness are most clearly seen (Ps. 77:16-20).

Chapter 10

Jacob's encounter with the Angel of God, the preincarnate Christ, reveals what is necessary for Jacob to be changed to Israel. Notice in Gen. 32:22-23 that Jacob sent on ahead what was precious to him. Jabbok signifies "emptying." Why is that an appropriate name for the place of a struggle such as Jacob experienced?

Jacob was left alone in God's presence (v. 24). Many

do not want to be alone with God. They might learn what He thinks about them. It really doesn't matter what anyone else thinks about us. The great question is, "What does God think?" We hear the answer to this question only when we separate ourselves from others' opinions, even our own thoughts and reasoning and allow the Spirit to show us what He sees.

God knew Jacob must overcome his tendency to do things his own way. The dislocation of his hip was the sentence of death on his striving in natural ways. God was saying that the carnal striving of his previous wrestling was wrong, but He could end it. Now Jacob would no longer wrestle with the power of the flesh but by the power of faith and prayer.

As long as Jacob could use his own strength, he did. Notice that it took God's touch to change him. Jacob became Israel only with God's help. We cannot free ourselves from the sinful tendency. "Who will release and deliver me from [the shackles of] this body of death? O thank God! [He will!] through Jesus Christ" (Rom. 7:24-25, AMP.).

Notes

Preface

1. William Dyrness, *Themes in Old Testament Theology* (Downers Grove, Ill.: InterVarsity Press, 1979), 31.

Introduction

1. Dyrness, *Themes in Old Testament Theology,* 42.

2. Michael Horton, *In the Face of God: The Dangers and Delights of Spiritual Intimacy* (Nashville: Word Publishing, 1996), 14.

3. Ibid.

Chapter 1

1. Alfred Edersheim, *Bible History, Old Testament* (reprint; Grand Rapids: William B. Eerdmans Publishing Co., 1975), 2:84.

2. Abraham Cohen, *Everyman's Talmud: The Major Teachings of the Rabbinic Sages* (New York: Schocken Books, 1949), 41.

3. Ibid., 42.

4. Daniel Steele, *Jesus Exultant* (Christian Witness Co., 1899; reprint, Salem, Ohio: Convention Book Store, n.d.), 152.

5. Ibid., 155.

Chapter 2

1. Nathan J. Stone, *Names of God* (Chicago: Moody Press, 1944), 25-27.

2. Hannah Whitall Smith, *The God of All Comfort* (Chicago: Moody Press, 1956), 95.

3. Elaine Hardt, "The Gift I Chose," *Women Alive!* March/April 1992, 9.

4. Dyrness, *Themes in Old Testament Theology,* 34.

5. Elizabeth Sherrill, "Closer to Him," *Guideposts,* June 2000, 35.

6. An Unknown Christian, *The Glory Christian* (London: Marshall Brothers, n.d.), 90.

Chapter 3

1. Harriet Louise Patterson, *Around the Mediterranean with My Bible* (Boston: W. A. Wilde Co., n.d.), 142-43.

2. P. P. Bilhorn, "Sweet Peace, the Gift of God's Love," *Songs of the Sanctuary* (Kansas City: Lillenas, n.d.), 210.

3. George D. Watson, *Our Own God* (Salem, Ohio: Schmul Publishing Co., 1992), 26.

4. A. W. Tozer, *Knowledge of the Holy* (San Francisco: HarperSanFrancisco, 1961), 100-101.

Chapter 4

1. R. C. Trench, *Notes on the Miracles of Our Lord* (Grand Rapids: Baker Book House, 1949), 164.

2. Haldor Lillenas, "Where They Need No Sun," *Songs of the Sanctuary,* 58.

Chapter 5

1. Trench, *Notes on the Miracles,* 67.

2. R. E. Carroll, *High Conceptions of God* (Salem, Ohio: Allegheny Publications, 1989), 65.

3. Ibid., 72.

4. Thomas L. Trevethan, *The Beauty of God's Holiness* (Downers Grove, Ill.: InterVarsity Press, 1995), 39.

5. E. N. Kirk, *The Word of Promise* (Salem, Ohio: Schmul Publishers), 15.

Chapter 6

1. Linda Hardin, "God Is Singing Over Me!" *Women Alive!* March/April 1998, 20.

2. John Piper, *The Pleasures of God* (Portland, Oreg.: Multnomah, 1991), 85.

3. William Clarke, quoted by H. Orton Wiley, *Christian Theology* (Kansas City: Beacon Hill Press, 1943), 3:378.

4. Quoted in Paul M. Bassett and William M. Greathouse, *Exploring Christian Holiness,* vol. 2, *The Historical Development* (Kansas City: Beacon Hill Press of Kansas City, 1985), 120.

5. Albert B. Simpson, *The Christ in the Bible Commentary* (Camp Hill, Pa.: Christian Publications, 1992), 1:39.

6. Andrew Murray, *God's Best Secrets* (Grand Rapids: Zondervan Publishing House, 1986), Mar. 31.

Chapter 7

1. Trevethan, *Beauty of God's Holiness,* 97.

2. Dr. Laura Schlessinger and Rabbi Stewart Vogel, *The Ten Commandments* (New York: HarperPerennial, 1999), 182.

3. Trevethan, *Beauty of God's Holiness,* 96.

Chapter 8

1. G. Campbell Morgan, *Studies in the Four Gospels: The Gospel According to Luke* (Old Tappan, N.J.: Fleming H. Revell Co., 1931), 182.

2. *His Victorious Indwelling: Daily Devotions for a Deeper Christian Life,* ed. Nick Harrison (Grand Rapids: Zondervan Publishing House, 1992), 340.

3. R. A. Torrey, *How to Pray* (Westwood, N.J.: Barbour and Co., 1989), 13.

Chapter 9

1. David H. Levy, *The Nature Company Guides: Skywatching* (San Francisco: Time-Life Books, 1999), 28.

2. Carroll, *High Conceptions of God,* 82.

3. Ibid., 39.

4. Levy, *Nature Company Guides,* 28.

Chapter 10

1. John N. Oswalt, *The Book of Isaiah, Chapters 40-66, The New International Commentary on the Old Testament* (Grand Rapids: William B. Eerdmans Publishing Co., 1998), 192.

2. Simpson, *Christ in the Bible Commentary,* 5:471.

3. *The Torah: A Modern Commentary,* ed. W. Gunther Plaut (New York: Union of American Hebrew Congregations, 1981), 221.

4. Ibid., 223.

5. Caroline M. Noel, "At the Name of Jesus," *Sing to the Lord* (Kansas City: Lillenas Publishing Co., 1993), 277.

6. *The Wesley Bible* (Nashville: Thomas Nelson, 1990), 889.

Appendix

1. Clarence W. Hall, *Samuel Logan Brengle: Portrait of a Prophet* (Chicago: Salvation Army Supply and Purchasing Dept., 1933), 225.

Additional Chapter Comments

1. Brennan Manning, *Reflections for Ragamuffins* (New York: HarperCollins, 1997), 184.

2. Joachim Neander, "Praise to the Lord, the Almighty," *Sing to the Lord,* 20.

3. Carroll, *High Conceptions of God,* 79.